Poetry and Prayer

Poetry and Prayer

Richard Griffiths

LONDON • NEW YORK

Continuum

The Tower Building   15 East 26th Street
11 York Road   New York
London SE1 7NX   NY 10010

www.continuumbooks.com

First published 2005

British Library Cataloguing-in-Publication Data
A catalogue record for this book is available from the British Library.

ISBN 0–8264–8158–2

Typeset by Fakenham Photosetting Limited
Fakenham Norfolk
Printed and bound by MPG Books Ltd,
Bodmin, Cornwall

To the Memory of

Penry Evans
Louis Massignon
Alec Vidler
Nicholas Zernov
Masters and friends

Contents

Foreword

Poetry and prayer are akin. Collections of hymns are found at least as early as the fourth century and probably earlier, and then move through the centuries to our own age. Not all persons who try their hand at what they think is poetry can be called poets; we define such people whose poetry is inferior as poetasters or rhymesters. Yet in religion we are not usually engaged with literary sensibility but with aspiration after ideals, and may treat authors, whose taste is imperfect, with a broad respect. Something spoke to that writer in the inner soul, and the words that came out might help our own minds towards understanding. Poetry struggles to express what cannot be written down in prose. Religion reaches up towards mysteries which are hardly definable. They need each other.

Richard Griffiths has dared to take the central moment of Christian faith, full of suffering but nevertheless of hope, and illuminate its sequence from great literature. For this task he has a rare qualification; of course the indispensable, a perception of the nature and mystery of faith; but also he is as familiar with French religious poetry as he is with English, and adds to that, through his origin in Wales and his residence there, the ability to enter into the power of lyrics in the Welsh tradition.

Of his poets who take us upward, probably the earliest of his Welsh authors, Henry Vaughan, is the most inspiring. For Vaughan had the qualities which religious poetry must share if it is to be authentic and neither rhetorical nor sentimental. The first quality is that of directness of vision – 'I saw Eternity the other night'. The second is akin to directness, a simplicity which may be that of innocence as in a child's mind. The third, though it seems hardly compatible with a childlike innocence, is a knowledge, somehow, somewhere, of suffering – we do not know the cause of this in Henry Vaughan, although scholars have guessed that it was the death of a brother who was close to him in affection. And the fourth is the sense that these words, even if they are personal and private to their author, touch a depth not in one person only but in humanity. The 'Stabat Mater', of Mary grieving beneath the cross, touches not only her but every mother who lost her child in its cradle, or in a car crash, or in Aberfan.

It is notorious that anyone who analyses a great poem is in danger. The pejorative phrase 'Eng. Lit.' means bodies of people who turn inspiration into pedestrian cluttered prose. But when we read Richard Griffiths we find not only a mind with a knowledge of suffering, but one that makes us think, and think again, of great poems and their meaning, and then of the texts of the New Testament which they seek to illuminate. Many will find much to lead their minds upwards in this profound meditation on religious souls' understanding of the gospel.

The Revd Professor Owen Chadwick

Preface

This book originated in a series of talks I had been giving, in parishes and elsewhere, about the usefulness of poetry as a stimulus for meditation and prayer. This experience led me to believe that there was a place for a book on this theme.

Theologians, and literary critics, may find much to disappoint them here. They are not, however, the readership for whom this book is intended. Although theology is naturally involved in the venture, and although literary critical techniques are central to it, everything has been done to try to make the book accessible to all thinking Christians. For this reason, technical words or phrases are as far as possible avoided. When they are needed, they are explained on the spot, within the text, and not relegated to inaccessible glossaries. Similarly, short notes on each poet are given in the text where the first major poem by him or her occurs, and not stowed away either in lengthy footnotes or in a special appendix.

Biblical quotations are on the whole taken from the Authorized Version of the Bible, because it was the text used by many of these poets. This is not in all cases the most accurate translation to use; but where a problem arises, reference is made to more modern translations, or (in the case of Catholic authors) to other contemporary translations. Using the Authorized Version, however, enables us to pick up biblical allusions in the poetry more clearly.

The method used is that of 'close reading', a technique which, amid all the changing fashions in literary criticism, still has its place. In the context of the Christian poets we will be looking at in this volume, it enables us to explore all the allusions in what are often, despite a simple appearance, highly complicated and suggestive texts. This can then open out new pathways for thought, prayer and meditation.

The first section of the book is a general examination of the nature of prayer, and of the place of the arts in general, and poetry in particular, in the Christian experience. There follow, in the central section, two sequences of subjects for meditation, each subject within each sequence being treated through the examination of an individual poem, or in some cases two poems. In each case, after an initial discussion of the poem, there follows a section entitled 'Reflections', which opens out areas for thought and prayer.

These sequences could serve either as stimuli for private prayer, or as a basis for Lenten devotions, or for discussion in Lent groups. Or they can just be dipped into – on a 'pick and mix' basis. The first sequence consists of eight medita-tions on the Crucifixion and Resurrection, the second of three meditations on the Christmas season. The final section of the book, consisting of four chapters, deals with certain central areas of Christian experience, from the joy of God in nature, through the problems of suffering and the despair of doubt, to the supportive arms of God's love for humankind.

I am grateful to a great many people for help and advice at various stages. I would like just to single out a few. Odette de Mourgues and Alison Fairlie introduced me to 'close reading' and have been an influence on my approach to literature ever since. Richard Harries, Vincent Strudwick, Leslie Griffiths and the late Ronald Thomas himself have stimulated me to thought on R.S. Thomas, and on the relationship between religion and the arts. John Furber, Pierre Glaudes, André Guyaux, Bernard Howells, Michael Jaffé, John Jolliffe, Henry Lefai, Dominique Millet, Edward Norman, Bernard Swift, Derrick Turner, Dilwyn Thomas, Peter Thomas and Wynn Thomas are among those with whom I have had fruitful discussions about Christian literature and Christian art. Two very special mentions must be made. Firstly, I learned a great deal about the relationship between art and religion from the conversation and writings of Pie Duployé, OP, a Dominican scholar I met in the 1960s. Everyone who met him will remember not only his colourful and often eccentric personality, but also the warmth of his friendship and the profundity of his thought, often hidden behind a barrage of flippant *boutades*. Secondly, there is Michael (Mick) Quinn. While this book was in the course of preparation, I received from Mick, an old friend of many years' standing, a copy of his superb little privately printed book entitled *Covenant with Silence*, in which he examines a number of poems, very much from the same perspective as I have been doing.[1] Two of the poems were ones (Edwin Muir's 'The Annunciation' and T.S. Eliot's 'Journey of the Magi') which I too had intended to treat. When I saw what Mick had made of them, I felt I could not compete, and so chose other poems instead.

Once one starts thinking about a series of themes, relevant information and ideas seem to come at you from every direction. Thus it is that I am indebted to Melvyn Bragg's Thursday morning programme 'In Our Time' for ideas on utopias and dystopias which now figure in my chapter on suffering; to a performance by the choir of King's College London of Peter Warlock's 'Bethlehem

1. Michael Quinn, *Covenant with Silence*, n.d. [2005]

Down' for the revelation of Bruce Blunt's poem of that name; and to Dominic Walker and John Lewis for ideas they put forward, one in a talk, the other in a sermon, on the joy of Good Friday.

Thanks are due to the following people for permission to reproduce copyright poems: to Emyr Humphreys for his poem 'The Serpent'; to Professor Geraint Gruffydd (Saunders Lewis's literary executor) and to Professor Gwyn Thomas for Gwyn Thomas's translation of Saunders Lewis's 'To the Good Thief'; to Gwydion Thomas for two poems by his father, R.S. Thomas; to Oxford University Press for two poems, and one stanza of another, by David Gascoyne; and to Professor Norma Rinsler of *Modern Poetry in Translation* and the translators Chana Bloch and Chana Kronfeld for their translation of Yehuda Amichai's 'And there are days' (first published in *Modern Poetry in Translation*, New Series, No. 14 (*Palestinian and Israeli Poets*), Winter 1998–99). Boosey and Hawkes, the publishers of 'Bethlehem Down', have been unable to find any details of Bruce Blunt's copyright heirs. If any heir should see this, could he or she please get in touch with me.

I am deeply grateful to Owen Chadwick, my former Master and a friend for over 45 years, for the foreword he has written for this volume. I am very much indebted to Robin Baird-Smith, of Continuum, for the faith he has shown in this venture. And above all, I must thank my wife Patricia for reading the work in progress, for making many perspicacious comments, and for putting up with me as I cut myself off from the household and battled with my text.

Lastly, the dedicatees. The poetry in this book comes from a great variety of Christian traditions, and the book is therefore dedicated to the memory of four men who, each in his way, helped me to understand those traditions. Firstly, my great-uncle A. Penry Evans, an outstanding Welsh Congregationalist preacher. Then Louis Massignon, a central figure in the Roman Catholic Church in France in the first half of the twentieth century, of whom I saw much in his final years. Then Alec Vidler, the Anglican theologian, who did so much to make me challenge my own assumptions about the Christian faith. And finally, Nicholas Zernov, who devoted his life to promoting understanding between the Orthodox and Anglican churches, and who made me a member of his Fellowship of St Alban and St Sergius. To all four I owe much.

Richard Griffiths
Penarth, 2005

SECTION ONE

INTRODUCTORY

CHAPTER ONE

Prayer

A friend of mine, who was dying, said to me: 'I've been trying to pray all my life. But it never seems to work. It's probably a bit late to learn, but tell me: how should I pray?'

The question was a vast one. My reply could not realistically address it in full. But he made me think, more deeply than I ever had before, about the reasons why so many of us have problems with prayer. Many of these appear to stem from a confusion between public and private prayer, and the carrying-over of the use of words from one to the other.

Public prayer

Public prayer is a vital part of the Christian life. In it, we come together as the Body of Christ. Though we are all individuals, we are all members of that Body. We differ in the way that the limbs of the body differ from each other. But that does not prevent us from being one coherent whole; and communal worship represents that wholeness.

By its nature, therefore, communal worship has to be uttered publicly. It has to have a form. It has to use words.

And very often, the impact of a public prayer or intercession depends upon the form that it takes.

Sometimes, it is the familiarity of the words that has the greatest impact upon the individuals of whom a congregation is made up. It is far too easy, when we are considering reform of the liturgy, to forget or neglect the importance of the known. The liturgy can be a strength and a support by its very familiarity. Indeed, amid the many distractions that assail every member of a congregation, it can be a guiding framework to which even the most inattentive can return. Whether we like it or not, events and problems from our own lives can distract us when we are in church. But, when we are praying as the Body of Christ, the actual form of the worship can take over, and a congregation, made up of some who are attending, and some who are not, is *as a whole* a prayerful body. Those parts of the liturgy, therefore, which are said by all should on the whole be familiar to all (this does not mean that you should never have anything new; but it does mean that the new needs to become a new norm of familiarity). Such set prayers can take on a life of their own, particularly when we bear in mind that we are sharing them not only with the congregation in which we are, but also with many other congregations throughout the land.

Within the prayers and intercessions said by an individual, and listened to by many, however, it is often the originality of wording that can have the greatest effect. Into the familiar framework of the liturgy, it is important that originality and excitement should be inserted. It is also essential to pray about matters of the day, those things that are present in everyone's minds. The impact of a prayer may be because of the thought-content; but the form in which that thought-content is clothed is also important. The most successful formal prayers and intercessions are those in which content and form fuse in an original and satisfying way. Often it is unusual but apt imagery that creates the effect; sometimes it is the shape of the sentences, the subtle uses of repetition, the carrying-along of the listener on a wave of language. Successful formal prayers are, like poetry, works of art – but works of art created for a specific purpose, that of inspiring and involving those who hear them, and bringing them closer to God.

Another form of prayer, that has become very popular of recent years, is extempore prayer. This is attractive to many. It is believed that through it the Spirit can speak directly not only to the congregation but also to the minister himself or herself. This, in the hands of a competent and confident improviser, can often be very effective. But there are dangers when a less confident or capable person undertakes this form of prayer. Only too often, it can become very repetitive, with the words 'Thank you, Lord ...' becoming an insistent refrain, which can give an impression of self-indulgence and of unconcern for coherence of content.

What all these public prayers have in common is that, by their nature, they rely on words, because in such prayer we are in communication not just with God but also with each other, and because words are the usual way in which we can do this. This is essentially what differentiates public prayer from private prayer.

Private prayer

One of the problems we have with private prayer is that we are not sure what form our prayers should take. Only too often, in imitation of our communal prayers in church, we feel constrained to put too much into words. Many of us have been conditioned into that from childhood onwards. How many of us, having recited parrot-fashion some set prayers at our bedside in our childhood – usually the Lord's Prayer plus a catch-all prayer containing our parents, our near relatives, and ending with asking that we should be 'good boys' (or girls) for our parents – continued using the same prayers well into our adolescence and adulthood, reciting them automatically, even when some details were completely out of date?

Yet private prayer has little need of words. As T.S. Eliot, in his poem 'Little Gidding', says:

> And prayer is more
> Than an order of words, the conscious occupation
> Of the praying mind, or the sound of the voice praying.

How often, we seem to feel that we have to *talk* to God. Amid the welter of words of which our prayer can consist, it sometimes seems as though God is being 'talked at' rather than 'talked with'. And it is hardly surprising that if we pray like this we expect a conversation in worldly terms, and therefore feel that we cannot 'hear' God, that we are talking into emptiness, with our words becoming no more than vain repetitions. In this way, when we most want to pray, when we are in sorrow or distress, the need to use words becomes a barrier between us and God, so that we do not find him in our distress. This is when we say that our prayer 'does not work', as though it were some kind of domestic machine which had broken down. But perhaps it is because we are trying so hard to make it 'work' that it fails to do so. We are expecting God to reply to us, as though this were a conversation in worldly terms. We are disappointed when we do not 'get a reply'. Perhaps we are expecting the wrong things.

Even in the area of prayer which would most seem to need words, petitionary prayer, in which we pray for specific things for ourselves or for others, words are little needed – indeed, the desire to put such prayers into precise words can often lead us into the wrong kind of prayer. Petitionary prayer should, of course, not be for an exact outcome, in that every prayer should have as its touchstone Christ's words in his prayer in Gethsemane: 'Nevertheless, not my will, but thine, be done.' When we pray for someone who is ill, therefore, we are praying for God's will to be done; for the person to recover or, if he or she does not recover, to be helped to bear their burden with fortitude. How much easier, in private prayer, just to bring that person before God, visualizing their condition, asking for God's help implicitly by our act of bringing them before him. The complications into which our prayer would otherwise become engulfed are thus simplified, and our prayer becomes easier.

The centre of private prayer is, however, not the bringing of petitions, but the forging of a relationship with God. How can we learn to pray in this way? How can we create that true relationship with God, which does not need questions and answers, does not need to pretend to be a human conversation? Only by finding a way through to this can we forge a foundation from which we can face the troubles of this world. We can be helped, in this quest, by looking at the experience of those medieval mystics who devoted their lives to prayer. For them, 'prayer' and 'meditation' were very closely linked. The 'words' of prayer rarely seem to be mentioned in their accounts of their experiences.

It is all summed up by the words of Psalm 46: 'Be still, and know that I am God.' Knowledge of God comes, not through intellectual arguments, or precise reasoning. It comes through the *experience* of God. And that experience, that knowledge, comes through calmness, stillness, receptiveness, trust. We must try not to be too 'busy' in our approaches to God. We must lay ourselves open to his presence.

There is a marvellous story, which may or may not be true. But, like most good stories of its type, it ought to be true, even if it isn't. It concerns a country priest who, coming to his church every morning, saw a simple farmworker there. Each day he stayed sitting there, for about half an hour, before he started work. One day the priest asked him how he prayed. 'Pray?' the man said. 'Don't do anything like that. I'm just there, and God's there. And he knows I'm there, and I know he's there.' That man was praying, even if he didn't realize it. And he was praying in one of the most effective ways possible.

When we start praying in this way, we must not necessarily expect to experience anything immediately. Gradually, however, through our growing sense of peace, of relief from the stresses of the world, of consolation from grief, of refreshment and renewal, we will have the surest sign of God's presence with us.

In the poetry of the Welsh priest-poet R.S. Thomas we are continually told that we must not go out to force God to listen to us and to reply. Patiently, we must wait, and he will come:

> The one eloquence
> to master is that
> of the bowed head, the bent
> knee, waiting.

(R.S. Thomas, 'Waiting')

Such silent prayer does not consist, however, of the attempt, as in the trances of Zen Buddhism, to extinguish all thoughts in our minds, to make ourselves 'like a plank of wood', open to the outside influences of a power that will enter into that vacated space. Christian private prayer is a conscious exercise, just as much as if we were composing verbal prayers. It is for this reason that preparation for prayer is so important. Such preparation can consist of the mental repetition of a simple phrase, which concentrates on one aspect of our Christian experience, such as penitence in the 'Jesus prayer' used by the Orthodox Church: 'Lord Jesus Christ, Son of God, have mercy upon me, a miserable sinner.' It can also consist of using an object, or a work of art, as a starting point for meditation. This latter is particularly useful for those of us who find that the attempt to pray without words can be almost as difficult as more verbal forms of prayer. A preliminary meditation, whether in front of a visual image, a Christian work of art, or when listening to music, or when stimulated by a piece of Christian poetry, can be the best way to lead in to our prayer.

Music, the visual arts, poetry, are all things which suggest, which half state, which hint at greater meanings behind their surface appearance. They can lead us into new ways of thinking and feeling, and at the same time can give us a glimpse of the glory of God, that mysterious glory which is half-hidden behind material reality, and which the ordinary non-poetic use of the words of prose can never hope to reach. In the next chapter, we will briefly look at the role of the arts, and specifically of poetry, in this quest.

*　　*　　*

All this is what I would have liked to say to my dying friend. All I was able to give was a short attempt at simple explanation. He was coming in and out of consciousness. But when I said: 'Be still, and know that I am God', he smiled seraphically, and said the one word: 'Know'.

CHAPTER TWO

Poetry

Art is a mystery. Through great art, we are vouchsafed high moments of experience which are inexplicable in material terms. When a shiver goes down our spine as we listen to a piece of music, when we pause to marvel at a great painting, when a poet's words take us outside the world of logical prose into something more rare, more intuitive, then we gain some kind of insight into a world beyond the material world around us. Philosophers, throughout the ages, whether Christian or not, have tried to define what that mysterious essence may be. Christian philosophers have seen it as a kind of fleeting insight into God's being, one of those 'reflections' of which St Paul speaks in the famous passage from his First Epistle to the Corinthians:

> Now we see only reflections in a mirror, mere riddles, but then we shall be seeing face to face. Now, I can only know imperfectly; but then I shall know just as fully as I am myself known.
>
> (1 Corinthians 13.12)

In this world of ours, the mysterious nature of God can only be half perceived. Only later, at the end of time, will we be able to see 'face to face'. Among those things which can nevertheless, in this world, give insight into God's being, we must count the revelation of God in the arts. The experience of nature can give us the same kind of revelation.

Music, because it does not even deal in words, is of course a prime example of the mysterious power of what we call the 'aesthetic experience'. The visual arts, similarly. It is when we look at poetry, however, that the achievement of this mysterious power becomes, at first, even more difficult to understand. In poetry, we are dealing with words, which of themselves have a meaning, or a series of meanings, closely related to the material reality around us. Surely here, on this basis, the sense of mystery would be harder to achieve?

Yet examine your own experience. The reading of a poem by a great poet can convey just the same sense of joy, of illumination, of unexplained sensations, as does a great piece of music. Yet the very same words and phrases that the poet has used could, if strung together in prose, convey clear, logical messages on the level of our conscious intellect. What is it, in poetry, that combines these same material bricks in such a way as to make a far more mysterious construction?

Speaking prosaically, one would say that it is, of course, the way in which images are used, the way in which surprising and compelling juxtapositions of images and ideas are produced, the way in which poetry cuts across the logical processes of prose. But this is merely to take the question one stage further. Why do these processes produce the effect that they do?

The answer, surely, is that only by such methods can the inexpressible be expressed – by images, by similes, by

12

metaphors, by allusions. As the poet R.S. Thomas has said, 'How shall we attempt to describe or express ultimate reality except through metaphor and symbol?'[2] Echoing Keats, Thomas has described elsewhere the poet's ability to be 'in uncertainties, mysteries, doubts, without any irritable reaching after fact and reason'.[3] As we shall see later in this volume, 'uncertainties', 'doubts', are often the only ways to win through to a solid faith, in which paradoxically nothing can be certain.

So poetry, using the same bricks as prose, creates a completely different building. The same words that prose uses so pointlessly can be transformed when they are used in poetry, where they are neither obscured nor constrained by the norms of logical discourse. In his poem 'After Jericho', R.S. Thomas sees words as needing to be resisted by words. One lot of words, those of prose, produce the 'aggression of fact'. Verse 'fights language with its own tools'. The poet blows his trumpet, like Joshua's army marching around Jericho, and, just as their trumpets destroyed the city's walls, creates 'the ruin of a vocabulary'. The words of prose are merely a 'conscript army'. The words of poetry are 'volunteers':

> There is an aggression of fact
> to be resisted successfully
> only in verse, that fights language
> with its own tools. Smile, poet,

---

2. R.S. Thomas, 'A Frame for Poetry', *The Times Literary Supplement*, 3 March 1966.
3. R.S. Thomas, Introduction to *The Penguin Book of Religious Verse*, 1963.

among the ruins of a vocabulary
you blew your trumpet against.
It was a conscript army; your words,
every one of them, are volunteers.

(R.S. Thomas, 'After Jericho')

Because of all these characteristics, poetry is a perfect vehicle for meditation. A piece of prose, in which everything tends to be very cut and dried, cannot have the same effect (unless it is a piece of highly 'poetic prose'). In a good poem, the mind is often taken several ways at the same time, as allusions and overtones enrich the subject matter, and multiple meanings emerge.

Note the phrase 'in a good poem'. Only in the highest examples of the poet's art do we find these riches.

★   ★   ★

This brings us to 'Christian art'. From what we have already seen, it is clear that all great art can be seen as implicitly Christian. But if all good art is Christian, not all 'Christian' art is good. There are three dangers it finds difficult to avoid, whether in the visual arts, in music, or in poetry. They are sentimentality, piety and banality.

Those dangers are often triggered by excessive self-consciousness in the Christian artist. The Dominican Pie Duployé once described the process:

Christian consciousness still claims to know this world, but it makes of it a clerical version. It will never know that moment of entire gratuity, when the object is considered and loved for itself; instead it will use that object prematurely for its own exclusive ends, which are the construction of the Kingdom of God, or (alas) what it believes to be the Kingdom of God. On this diet, a Christian consciousness will absorb everything: there is no art so tough that it will not end up by neutralising and annexing it, but at what a price![4]

The sentimental tendencies that can bedevil such art, whether in the visual arts, or music, or poetry, are well described by the Swiss artist Alexandre Cingria, writing in the early twentieth century about the visual arts in an essay entitled 'The Decadence of Sacred Art':

There is a truly diabolical art which consists of aping beauty. This art gains the approval of almost all the Christian public, by a certain prettiness, by a poetic appearance, by a surface polish which conceals, from insensitive, lazy eyes, a complete absence of life, intelligence and beauty. [Certain Christian pictures] seem touching because they are supposed to be depicting episodes in the life of our Lord or the Virgin Mary, and because they translate them into a style generally attributed to the joys of maternity or of sentimental love. This art is all lies. It borrows, from the legend which is printed under the image, the admiration and the veneration which should be given to the image itself. It is by this art that the Devil enslaves Christians, and prevents them from honouring God as he should be honoured.[5]

4. Pie Duployé, OP, *La Littérature dans le Royaume de Dieu* (Paris: Bibliothèque de l'Homme d'Action, 1961), p. 18.
5. Alexandre Cingria, *La Décadence de l'art sacré* (Paris: Bibliothèque de l'Art Catholique, 1919), pp. 38–40.

We should not necessarily despise such art, however, even if we should beware it. Norman Nicholson, in the Introduction to his 1942 *Anthology of Religious Verse, Designed for the times*, describes the kind of Christian poetry which is only too common (and which he was not going to use in his anthology) thus:

> Many people think of 'Religious Poetry' as moral uplift in rhyme or pious verse about the Good Shepherd – the literary equivalent of the pictures distributed by Sunday Schools at Christmas and Easter. There is no need to despise such verse or to doubt the sincerity of those who write it or enjoy it, but, to the more critical reader, the use of conventional images and worn-out phrases seems to imply that Christianity itself is no longer a living thing.[6]

Alongside such religious art, however (as Nicholson was to show in his anthology) there is a robust tradition of Christian art which can vie with the best art of the secular tradition. There are, for example, the stark paintings of the Crucifixion by Grünewald. There are the Bach B minor Mass and the St Matthew Passion. There are the superb icons of the Orthodox tradition, so perfect as a source of Christian meditation. And there is a vast amount of highly charged Christian poetry, of great literary value, which similarly forms a perfect basis for meditation upon the great themes of our faith. These works of art, these poems, conform to the highest standards of artistic creation. They are appreciable by everyone, Christians and non-Christians alike, though their subject matter makes them of particular interest to Christians.

6. Norman Nicholson, Introduction to *An Anthology of Religious Verse, Designed for the times* (London: Pelican Books, 1942).

In them the Christian faith is not diminished, as in so much other Christian art, but enhanced and illuminated.

★ ★ ★

What Christian poetry should we use in this volume, then? One would be tempted to say, if one was looking merely at the banal and sentimental material of which so much Christian poetry is made up, that one should give up the idea. Because good poetry, whether religious or not, can be the basis for religious meditation (in that through the poet's art we gain a glimpse into the ineffable), perhaps it would be worth just using good secular poetry. But there is, as we have seen, a great deal of Christian poetry which is also great poetry, and which can stand comparison with the greatest of secular poetry. We have an array of Christian poets, from the sixteenth century to the present, whose writings fully repay close reading, and reach out to the ultimate as all good poetry is able to do, while also treating central Christian themes. No need, then, for lack of Christian resources, to have recourse in a volume like this to secular poetry (though it would be interesting at another time to produce such a volume, in which secular poetry could be used as a basis for Christian meditation).

The poems which we will be reading in the succeeding pages are taken from all periods, and from many different areas of Christian experience, from Nonconformism to Roman Catholicism, via the Anglican Church. They have been chosen for the way in which they take us beyond the banal statement of the obvious, and force us to think again about our Christian faith.

It may seem strange, in a book which stresses the need to get away from words in private prayer, to have written so

17

many words on the subject. It is hoped, however, that once the reader has used this book to examine the examples of Christian poetry chosen here, he or she will be moved to look at other examples of their choice in the same way, without need of written commentary of this type.

In poetry, the Word speaks to us more directly than in any other form of verbal communication. It speaks to us directly, because, paradoxically, in ordinary human terms its discourse is indirect and allusive. It avoids the pitfalls of everyday communication, and speaks to us through silence. Faced by such a mystery, all we can do is marvel.

SECTION TWO

Meditations

CHAPTER THREE

Eight Meditations on the Crucifixion and Resurrection

A Lenten prologue

Sin and temptation

Like ivy climbing you wrapped your cunning about
The tender bark of the forbidden tree
Luring into its shade the naked lout
To sow the seed of Death in Arcady:
And away you slid, exultant, happy, hot
To spread your sticky poison like a trap
To catch his progeny: like the glossy knot
That punished Laocoon and the two sons in his lap.

In the wilderness you whistled after Another
And tried to hold him in your bold intelligent stare
But you in turn were transfixed. It was our Saviour
Who drew you to him, limp in the still air
Wound you about his body like a sculptured torque
To squeeze the poison from your lethal fork.

(Emyr Humphreys, 'The Serpent', adapted from Gwenallt's 'Y Sarff')

Emyr Humphreys (b. 1919) is Wales's leading novelist in the English language. He is also a remarkable poet. Brought up as an Anglican, and intended at one time for the priesthood, he was, through his marriage to his wife Elinor (a daughter of the manse), introduced to the world of Welsh Nonconformism, which has led, in his work, to what has been described as 'the moral questioning which arises naturally (if in these days infrequently) from the Nonconformist Wales of the past'.[7]

One of the major readings for Lent has always been the description of Jesus Christ's period of temptation in the wilderness, for 40 days immediately after his baptism in the Jordan by John the Baptist. It is seen as the necessary preparation for his mission. It has also been seen as a parallel to, and the answer to, the temptation of Adam and Eve in the Garden of Eden. Where the first inhabitants of this earth had been tempted, and had succumbed, Jesus underwent temptation and overcame it. In this he showed himself to be the 'second Adam' who would reverse the effects of the Fall that resulted from the first temptation, and annul the sentence passed on mankind as a result of the sin of the first Adam. In that sense, the temptation in the wilderness can be seen as the prologue to Christ's redeeming sacrifice at the Crucifixion.

This poem illustrates this parallel between the temptation of Adam and Eve and that of Christ by extending the image of the serpent of Eden into the later temptation. And what

7. Meic Stephens, *The Oxford Companion to the Literature of Wales* (Oxford: OUP, 1986), p. 272.

a serpent it is! Cunning, poisonous, intelligent. We see him 'wrapping his cunning' round the forbidden tree, slithering exultantly away once the bait has been taken, spreading his poison, and then, when it comes to Jesus, fixing him with his 'bold intelligent stare'. The contrast between the two events lies in the adversaries he has chosen for himself: the 'naked lout' of Eden, an easy prey; and our Saviour, who masters him.

There is an interesting use, here, of classical parallels to the biblical story. Adam's sin brought death into the world of Eden; but here Eden is described as 'Arcady', the ideal region that the Greeks had seen as the place where the 'Golden Age' had been in existence, before humanity declined into its present state. It is therefore a fitting parallel to the biblical story; and indeed, in the writings of the Renaissance, the two myths were often intertwined.

The other classical parallel is that of Laocoon, of whom a remarkable statue, from classical times, has caught the imagination of modern man from the sixteenth century onwards. Laocoon was the Trojan priest who had angered Apollo by marrying and begetting children despite a vow of celibacy, and also by warning the Trojans against the wooden horse of the Greeks. Apollo sent two great sea serpents, which coiled themselves around Laocoon and his twin sons, and crushed all three to death. The famous statue of the three of them, struggling in the coils of the serpents, was created in about the second century BC, and well known in the ancient world; it was then lost to sight, but rediscovered in 1506, and is said to have had a great effect upon Michelangelo's art, and upon the European baroque in general. It became widely known, throughout Europe, through casts and engravings, as an exemplary portrayal of suffering and emotional anguish.

The poet has not, however, introduced Laocoon merely because these appear to him to be parallel stories to do with snakes. He sees a further parallel: the fact that all those descended from Adam were to be punished for their ancestor's fault, just as Laocoon's sons were for their father's. This is the central point of the poem, for it leads straight into the depiction of the serpent's meeting with the second Adam, and its defeat. Jesus is depicted as winding the snake 'about his body like a sculptured torque'. The reference once more to the Laocoon statue is obvious; but here, it is not the snakes which are squeezing a man to death, but a man, a God, who is 'squeezing the poison' from the snake.

Reflections

The parallel with the ancient gods draws our attention to one of the most troubling aspects of the story of the Fall of Man. We tend to look at the vengeful gods of the ancient Greeks, and deplore their methods, whereby the sins of the fathers were visited on the children, from generation to generation. Yet one of the major myths of the Christian religion seems to depend on the same arbitrary form of vengeance. Adam and Eve were tempted by the possibility of knowledge, the possibility of becoming 'like gods, knowing both good and evil'. They disobeyed God, and death came into the world, and man was no longer immortal. Sin came into the world. All humankind thenceforth would be intrinsically sinful; and suffering and sorrow would be their lot. The rest of humankind would therefore be suffering because of the acts of Adam and Eve. Where is the difference between that, and the arbitrary gods of the Greeks?

Perhaps it is better to look at the story for what it is. Like the story of the Creation, it appears to be an attempt to explain the nature of the world by use of a mythical story. Humankind has always wondered why there is so much suffering in the world, and why there is such evil. It has also wondered why, amid all this, human beings have within them an instinct to good, a 'conscience', which differentiates them from other animals. Adam and Eve's disobedience can be seen as a convenient explanation, in that they were created perfect, without knowledge of good and evil (or at any rate almost perfect, for they did have within them the seeds of disobedience), and evil came into the world through their fault. The story explains, also, why despite our sinful state we have instincts to good. It suggests that those instincts may be some kind of memory of our previous existence, some mark of the godlike that still remains hidden within us.

In both the story of the Garden of Eden, and the story of Jesus's temptation in the desert, the Devil (or the serpent) is described as an actual being, that tempts human beings. In other words, according to this interpretation of the world the Devil has a role separate from that of human beings. He exists in his own right. Evil thus becomes a force, an actual being, that engages in a kind of 'tug-of-war' with God for the fate of human beings. This has, of course, been one form of Christian belief over many centuries. The first prayer of Compline runs: 'Be sober, be watchful. Your adversary the devil prowls around like a roaring lion seeking someone to devour. Resist him, firm in your faith.' Yet there has always been, alongside this, a tradition that sees evil as coming from within, rather than from without (St Thomas Aquinas, for example, seeing evil as the absence of good). It is possible to see the concept of the Devil as having been a convenient hook on which to hang those human instincts to wrong that seem to sum up the nature of our imperfect world.

In the same way, in Jesus's time, it was believed that various forms of illness, and in particular mental illness, were caused by devils which 'possessed' people. In the words of Austin Farrer:

> Demonology was the child of scientific ignorance. It provided a language in which matters beyond the reach of contemporary science could be mythically described. It was better to ascribe the motives of madness to an infesting demon than to hold the unfortunate sufferer responsible for them.[8]

In speaking of such things, Jesus was surely just translating, into terms which his contemporaries would understand, far greater truths? When, for example, he portrays a man from whom a devil has been cast out being revisited by that selfsame devil after he has travelled far and wide, because that devil finds the place still empty (Luke 11. 24–26), isn't he just saying that it is no good giving up evil, one must also positively espouse good, or else one will decline into evil again? One thing is certain: the belief in devils being able to possess people has caused immeasurable harm over the ages, as recent events in relation to the treatment of children by certain evangelical sects have made clear.

We can each make up our own minds as to the view of the Devil that we wish to take. Is it an actual being, a positive force for evil? Or is it a convenient explanation for the intrinsic flaws in human nature, and for the temptations we undergo? Was Jesus's temptation in the desert a meeting, and a struggle, with an evil being, or a struggle with himself? He had taken on the being of a man; and it was essential to God's purpose that he should take on every aspect of humankind: its sufferings, its temptations. It would

---

8. Austin Farrer, *Love Almighty and Sins Unlimited* (New York: Doubleday, 1961), p. 128.

have been so easy to prove to everyone that he was Son of God, by throwing himself down from the pinnacle of the Temple, and being saved. He would thereby have saved himself all the suffering of his mission.

Whatever language we use to describe the state of humankind, and the temptations that continually beset us, there is little doubt that those temptations are very real, and that we need help to resist them. This is surely where Jesus comes in. As God, he had the power to resist all temptations, to 'squeeze the poison' out of them. Yet as a man, he went through the same stresses as we do, before triumphing over sin. Just as, through his suffering, he is there beside us, if we need him, in *our* suffering, so through the temptations he underwent he is able to be there beside us when we are tempted, helping us to overcome.

To give in to his temptations would have been to abort his mission. As it was, he was able to go on to the inevitable suffering of Calvary. In that sense, the temptation in the desert is a true prologue to the events of Good Friday.

Palm Sunday and Good Friday

Human frailty, divine forgiveness

It was but now their sounding clamours sung,
'Blessèd is he that comes from the Most High!'
And all the mountains with 'Hosanna!' rung;
And now, 'Away with Him – away!' they cry,
And nothing can be heard but 'Crucify!'
    It was but now, the crown itself they save,
      And golden name of King unto him gave;
And now, no King, but only Caesar, they will have.

It was but now they gatherèd blooming May,
And of his arms disrob'd the branching tree,
To strow with boughs and blossoms all Thy way,
And now the branchless trunk a cross for Thee,
And May, dismay'd, Thy coronet must be:
    It was but now they were so kind, to throw
    Their own best garments where Thy feet should go,
And now, Thyself they strip, and bleeding wounds they
    show.

See where the author of all life is dying.
O fearful day! He dead, what hope of living?
See where the hopes of all our lives are buying.
O cheerful day! They bought, what fear of grieving?
Love, love for hate, and death for life is giving:
    Lo, how his arms are stretched abroad to grace thee,
    And, as they open stand, call to embrace thee!
Why stay'st thou then, my soul; O fly, fly, thither, haste
    thee.

(Giles Fletcher, stanzas 32–34 of Christ's Victorie and Triumph
in Heaven and Earth)

Giles Fletcher (*c.* 1585–1623) was a Fellow of Trinity College, Cambridge, from 1605 to 1618, and Reader in Greek grammar and Greek language. He then became rector of Alderton, Suffolk. His greatest literary achievement, the long poem *Christ's Victorie and Triumph in Heaven and Earth, over and after Death,* was composed when he was at Trinity, and published in 1610. It has been suggested that Fletcher's verse was a source of influence for Milton. Certainly, its power (as witnessed by this extract) makes of him one of the more remarkable religious poets of his period, and a prime example of early Anglican spirituality.

Our celebration of Palm Sunday rests on a contrast. Five days before the events of Good Friday, we have a moment of apparent joy, as we commemorate Jesus's triumphant entry into Jerusalem, riding upon a donkey. The people had welcomed him ecstatically:

> And a very great multitude spread their garments in his way; others cut down branches from the trees, and strawed them in his way.
> And the multitudes that went before, and that followed, cried, saying, Hosanna to the Son of David: Blessed is he that cometh in the name of the Lord; Hosanna in the highest.

> (Matthew 21. 8–9)

This is a royal entry. The people's spreading of their clothes on the road on which he will pass is a sign of Christ's kingship, in the same way as, in the Old Testament, the people had done homage to Jehu by spreading their cloaks under him, shouting 'Jehu is king!' (2 Kings 9.13); and the crowd cries out that he is 'the Son of David', thus underlining the fact that he is entering his royal city. Even the phrase 'who comes in the name of the Lord' points to Jesus as King, as the phrase 'he that cometh' was a phrase denoting the Messiah (see, e.g., Psalm 118, 'Blessed be he that cometh in the name of the Lord').[9] Everything underlines his glory.

The crowd that called for Jesus's death on Good Friday was not, of course, necessarily made up of the same people who had welcomed him into Jerusalem the previous

---

9. For a discussion of these themes, see John Fenton's commentary, *St Matthew* (Penguin New Testament Commentaries, 1963).

Sunday. Fletcher, however, stresses the contrast between the events of the two days by taking it that these were the selfsame people, who had perhaps seen Jesus purely as an earthly Messiah, come to 'restore Israel', and had reacted against him thereafter, not realizing that his kingship is not of this world.

This is an emotional and highly charged text. The most striking thing about it is the change of mood between the first two stanzas and the last one. This change of mood is produced not just by the content, but also by the rhythm and language. In the first two stanzas the contrast in the people's attitude is pointed up by a whole number of powerful rhetorical procedures; and then all that measured comparison is blown apart by an ecstatic evocation of the immediacy of Christ's appeal to us, and of the poet's precipitate response, which plunges us into responding too, like him.

The first two stanzas underline the contrast by the insistent repetition of the words 'It was but now' (lines 1, 6, 9, 14), contrasted with 'and now' (lines 4, 8, 12, 16), at regular intervals. The first stanza uses the very words from the two moments in the Bible. 'It was but now', on Palm Sunday, that Christ had been welcomed into Jerusalem, with the people crying 'Blessed is he that cometh in the name of the Lord; Hosanna in the highest'; 'now', on Good Friday, they cry 'Away with him, away with him, crucify him.' Then, they had wanted him as king; now they say 'We have no king but Caesar' (John 19.15).

The second stanza makes the same contrast, but now in visual terms. The parallels are harsh. The boughs and blossoms they had strewn in his path, 'blooming May', make way for 'the branchless trunk' that is his Cross. In a typical early seventeenth-century use of a pun (which seems out of place to the modern eye), the awful change is further underlined, as we hear that 'May' is now 'dismay'd'. Then, these people had thrown their clothes before him; now he is stripped of his own clothes. Indeed, the contrast is made even stronger by the fact that the same people had 'disrobed' the May tree, and now 'strip' Christ.

At the end of that second stanza the stripping of Christ reveals his 'bleeding wounds'. From now on, it is as though that revelation of his suffering creates a complete change of mood in the poet, a change which is denoted by a sudden change of rhythm in the third stanza. Up to now, the contrast has been bitter, but orderly and argued in content, and calm in rhythm. Now, the immediacy of Christ's suffering, and the poet's own horrified reaction, are brought to us by the repetitions of the word 'See', by a series of rhetorical questions and exclamations, and by a new, disjointed rhythm. We, the readers, are now placed at the centre of the action, as we are urged to see what is going on, to see and understand what it all means, and to share the poet's reactions.

We are presented with a dramatic contrast. Jesus is God. God is the author of all life. But Jesus, God, is dying. We are told to 'see' this, and then the poet breaks out: 'O fearful day! He dead, what hope of living?' This is swiftly matched with the realization that Christ, through his sacrifice, has brought us hope of redemption: 'O cheerful day! They bought, what fear of grieving?' With the close repetition of the word 'Love' Fletcher now stresses Christ's gifts of love and life, and their triumph over hate and death. 'Love, love for hate, and death for life is giving.' And we are now pressed once more to look closely at the scene on the Cross, 'Lo . . .' Jesus's hands outstretched on the Cross are seen as being stretched out to bless us, but also, equally importantly, to embrace us with his love. In the final line, ecstatically, the poet asks why his soul is standing still, and calls on it, with the urgent repetition of 'Oh fly, fly' to hasten to Christ's embrace – and we, the readers, are implicitly exhorted to have the same reaction.

Reflections

This poem raises a number of matters central to the Christian experience. Firstly, there is the fickle nature of human reactions, as seen in the first two stanzas. We, too, are perpetually changeable in our attitudes, not only to the events of life around us, but also in our relationship with God. How often do we praise him in our prayers and worship in church, and then go out into the world and behave in a way that is entirely incompatible with Jesus's example? It is worth thinking about all that we have been doing day by day, and assessing what we would have felt if Jesus had come through the door as we were in the middle of doing it.

There is also the question of the meaning of the events of Good Friday themselves. In the third stanza, the poet gives us something of a surprise. When he has evoked the 'fearful day' of the Crucifixion, and asked 'he dead, what hope of living?', we would have expected this rhetorical question to have been answered by a reference to Easter Day, to Christ rising from the dead and giving us 'the hope of eternal life'. The answer is, however, more subtle than that. There is another message of Good Friday, one that is too often forgotten. This message is not one of gloom at Christ's death, followed on Easter Day by joy at his Resurrection. It is the deeper message that Good Friday itself is a day of joy, 'O cheerful day!', because Jesus's death on that day showed us that, whatever our sins, whatever our past, the God of love forgives us, and through that forgiveness enables us to go forward and lead our lives as he intended. Where the

Resurrection represents the triumph over physical death, Christ's sacrifice of love at the Crucifixion is the triumph over spiritual death, the death of sin. Christ has bought our hope of salvation, through his sacrifice.

This leads us to ponder on the mystery of Christ's love. Love is being exchanged for hate; he is prepared to save even those who hated him enough to bring about his death. His exhortation for us to love our enemies is here being lived out by Christ himself. Christ stretches out his arms, longing to embrace us all with his love. Yet it is not that simple. He holds out his arms, but the poet has to exhort his soul (and, by implication, ours) not to 'stay' or delay, but to 'hasten' to 'fly' to that embrace. In other words, much still depends on us. God has given us free will; only if we exert that free will by responding and entering his embrace will Christ's love be given to us. Our aspirations to good are helped by God's grace, but that grace is dependent on our acceptance of it.

This is all so difficult. How much easier it is to procrastinate, rather than 'hasten' to accept God's love! How often do we leave our prayers, how often do we leave the Eucharist, full of good intent, only to find ourselves distracted by the first mundane problem that crosses our path! We are like the people Lancelot Andrewes, the seventeenth-century divine, described in his famous Epiphany sermon (which was to form the basis for T.S. Eliot's poem 'The Journey of the Magi'). The wise men, said Andrewes, made haste the moment they saw the star. 'It was but *vidimus, venimus* with them, they *saw*, and *came*.' But what about us?

> And we, what would we have done? Sure, these men of the *East* shall *rise in judgment against the men of the West*, that is, us: and their *faith*, against ours, in this point. With them it was but *vidimus, venimus*. With us,

33

it would have been *veniemus* [we may come] at most. Our fashion is, to see and see again, before we stir a foot: Specially, if it be to the service of Christ. Come such a journey, at such a time? No: but fairly have put it off till the spring of the year, till the days longer, and the ways fairer, and the weather warmer: till better travelling to Christ. Our *Epiphany* would surely have fallen in *Easter-week* at the soonest.

Our hope must be that we may overcome our reluctance to commit ourselves, our inability to make the instinctive plunge that God requires of us; and that, by accepting God without afterthoughts, we ourselves may become worthy of acceptance by him.

Good Friday 1

Christ's suffering, and our own offering

When I survey the wondrous Cross
On which the Prince of Glory died,
My richest gain I count but loss,
And pour contempt on all my pride.

Forbid it, Lord, that I should boast
Save in the death of Christ, my God;
All the vain things that charm me most,
I sacrifice them to his blood.

See, from his head, his hands, his feet,
Sorrow and love flow mingled down;
Did e'er such love and sorrow meet?
Or thorns compose so rich a crown?

His dying crimson like a robe
Spreads o'er his body on the Tree,
Then am I dead to all the globe,
And all the globe is dead to me.

Were the whole realm of nature mine,
That were an offering far too small;
Love so amazing, so divine,
Demands my soul, my life, my all.

(Isaac Watts, from Hymns and Spiritual Songs)

Isaac Watts (1674–1748), son of a Nonconformist tradesman, was for many years pastor of the Independent Congregation in Mark Lane, London, before retiring early owing to ill health. In his *Hymns and Spiritual Songs* (1707, revised and enlarged in 1709), one finds some very well-known hymns, including 'O God, our help in ages past', 'Jesus shall reign where'er the sun', and, of course, 'When I survey'. Though often deceptively simple-seeming, many of these hymns are among the richest in our hymn books, and give evidence of a devout, lived faith.

This hymn is a vivid exploration of the mystery of Christ's suffering. In it we, the readers, are subtly drawn into the experience by a personal involvement in what is going on; we are led to imagine ourselves at the scene, as onlookers at the Passion of our Saviour.

The tone, and viewpoint, are crucial to the hymn's effect. It is not a poem of exhortation, where we are told what we should think, and what we should do. Far from ordering us to listen to a lesson, the poet depicts himself as undergoing the experience himself. We participate in his experience, as he stands there as our representative, looking at the Cross, wondering at Christ's sacrifice, and drawing from it a lesson for all humankind.

He impresses on us from the start his status as an observer, with the immediacy of the word 'I': '*When I survey* the wondrous Cross.' He then contrasts the fact that Christ is 'the Prince of Glory' with Christ's ignominious death on the Cross. This contrast is immediately paralleled with the similar contrasts it produces in the poet's (and our) life: 'My richest gain I count but loss'; and this is immediately followed by his emotional response: he does not just reject pride, he 'pours contempt' on it. This contrast between pride and humility is continued in the second stanza, where the only thing we can boast of is the fact of Christ's death, compared with which all the things that seem important to us in this world fade into insignificance, and must be sacrificed.

Up to this point, though we have been told that it is the poet's 'surveying' or contemplation of the Cross that has produced these thoughts, we have had no actual depiction of what he has been seeing. This is now led into by the idea of 'sacrifice'. The poet sacrifices the vain things of this world to Christ's *blood*. The image is an important one, which from now on will permeate the rest of the poem. Blood is a highly evocative word to use in relation to sacrifice, raising as it does the idea of Old Testament blood sacrifices, of which Jesus Christ's sacrifice is a continuation (and transformation), with it now being God himself who is being offered up, like the Paschal lamb that was traditionally sacrificed at the Jewish Passover. Jesus is 'the Lamb of God, which taketh away the sin of the world' (John 1.29).

As St Paul puts it, 'Christ our Passover is sacrificed for us' (1 Corinthians 5.7), and Christ has given himself up for us as 'a sacrifice to God for a sweetsmelling savour' (Ephesians 5.2). The image of blood is central to this belief. As the Epistle to the Hebrews puts it: 'Neither by the blood of goats and calves but by his own blood he entered in once into the holy place, having obtained eternal redemption for us' (Hebrews 9.12). In the words of Christ himself, as he instituted the communion service as a remembrance of his sacrifice, 'This is my blood of the new testament, which is shed for many for the remission of sins' (Matthew, 26.28).

The idea of blood is thus intimately linked with the idea of Christ's sacrifice. And by the way in which he uses this image, the poet stresses our participation in that sacrifice. 'I sacrifice them to his blood.' We *share* in Christ's sacrifice; as St Paul said, in words that are echoed in our communion service: 'The cup of blessing which we bless, is it not the communion of [or 'the sharing in'] the blood of Christ?' (1 Corinthians 10.16). The full meaning of that sharing will be brought out later in the poem.

Christians tend to take this blood imagery for granted. Non-religious people are at times shocked by what Richard Harries has described as 'the sacrificial, cannibalistic language of the Eucharist'.[10] It is important, however, to understand that in this context blood imagery is not shocking – it was chosen as the only image that can convey the reality of sacrifice, of suffering, of salvation.

At the beginning of stanza 3, we are dramatically brought back to the physical reality of the Cross, by the abrupt imperative 'See'. It is no longer merely the poet who is surveying the scene. We, his readers, are directly called upon to witness, with him, what is happening; and the idea of

10. Richard Harries, *God outside the Box* (London: SPCK, 2002) p. 113.

blood has been so powerfully introduced that the word itself does not even need to be used. Instead, the attributes of Christ's sacrifice, 'sorrow and love' are used in its place: 'See, from his head, his hands, his feet / Sorrow and love flow mingled down.'

We *see* the blood flowing from his head, hands and feet, but it is the meaning of that blood that Watts points to in the rhetorical questions we are then asked, with the words 'sorrow and love' being insistently repeated. The contrasts between glory and ignominy, which we heard in the first and second stanzas, are reiterated, but attached to another physical object, the crown of thorns: 'Did e'er such love and sorrow meet? / Or thorns compose so rich a crown?'

So blood, and the crown of thorns, are the physical, visual images that are used to point to the physicality of Christ's suffering, but also to the true meaning of this sacrifice. The thorns around Christ's brow are not just a sign of the ignominy of the Cross; the mockery that had been intended by them has rebounded on the mockers, for Christ *is* the King, and those thorns are a 'rich' crown. He is 'the Prince of Glory', even as he suffers on the Cross. And the sacrifice that has been made on our behalf is one composed of love for humankind, symbolized by Christ's blood.

Now we come to the moment of Christ's death; and blood is used once more, as a powerful image for his agony. 'His dying crimson' (note how once again blood is not mentioned directly) spreads over his body 'like a robe'. A crimson robe is, of course, a sign of royalty; so yet again the contrast is being drawn. Christ is King; his death cannot destroy that fact. But this is not earthly kingship; and the effect on the onlooker is to detach him from all earthly hopes, desires and ambitions; he is dead to the world, and the world is dead to him.

The final stanza sums up why this is so, and points us to

the future. 'Were the whole realm of nature mine . . .' We cannot offer anything matching Christ's sacrifice, but we as Christians share in that sacrifice, and must make an offering of some kind. All we have is ourselves. And God's amazing love, as seen in Christ's sacrifice, demands 'my soul, my life, my all'.

Reflections

This poem involves us directly in the reality, the horror and the pain of the Cross. It takes us to the scene, and we are there, with the poet, as observers of it. Our meditation here is bound to be emotion-centred, rather than thought-centred. Our emotional response leads us to imagine ourselves at the scene. For this, visual images may be of use to us. Not so much the sanitized versions of the Crucifixion produced by so many Renaissance artists, but pictures which give us a graphic impression of the actual physical sufferings of Christ in all their horror. Some of the best examples of this are the realistic paintings of Mathias Grünewald, as found in the altarpiece in the Isenheim Museum of Colmar. Something of the impression of these paintings is given by a passage from David Gascoyne's poem 'Ecce Homo':[11]

> Whose is this horrifying face,
> This putrid flesh, discoloured, flayed,
> Fed on by flies, scorched by the sun?
> Whose are these hollow red-filmed eyes
> And thorn-spiked head and spear-struck side?
> Behold the Man: He is Man's Son.

(David Gascoyne, 'Ecce Homo')

11. For a short profile of David Gascoyne, see p. 137.

Having imagined ourselves into the terrible situation of the Cross, we can then look back on Watts's hymn and understand more clearly the way in which he relates the Crucifixion to us, in our own lives, so that, with him, we feel that we want to translate that understanding into action. What Watts shows us is that, when we view, or 'survey' the Cross, we, unlike those who merely stood by at the scene, are inevitably led to ask ourselves, 'Should this affect the way I live?'

At the end of the Eucharist, when we have commemorated Christ's sacrifice, there is a final prayer (expressed in various forms in our various prayer books, but retaining always the same meaning) which admirably expresses the same idea. We say:

> We thank you, Father, for feeding us with the body and blood of your Son in this holy sacrament, through which we are assured of the hope of eternal life. We offer ourselves to you as a living sacrifice.

And the way in which we can offer ourselves is not merely by meditating upon Christ's sacrifice, or by worshipping within church, but by going out into the world to do Christ's work. That prayer ends: 'Send us out in the power of your Spirit to live and work to your praise and glory.'

That 'living and working' may be the bringing of help and succour to those in need, whether material or spiritual; it may be the prayer and the devotions of the contemplative life; it may be the 'Martha' role of providing practical help in a Christian community; it may be living through personal pain of mind or body; it may be just the living-out of the Christian life as an example to all those around one. The variety of roles is endless, but the essential thing is to do whatever one does for the glory of God, without thought of reward or acclaim, and without excessive and public piety.

Good Friday 2

Stabat Mater: love human and divine

Stabat Mater dolorosa,
juxta crucem lacrimosa,
dum pendebat Filius.

At the Cross her station keeping
stood the mournful Mother weeping, close to Jesus at the last.

Cujus animam gementem,
contristatam ac dolentem,
pertransivit gladius.

Through her soul, His sorrow sharing, all His bitter anguish bearing, now at length the sword has passed.

O quam tristis et afflicta
fuit illa benedicta
Mater Unigeniti.

O, how sad and sore distressed was the Mother, highly blest,of the sole-begotten One!

Quae moerebat et dolebat,
et tremebat, cum videbat
nati poenas inclyti.

Christ above in torment hangs, She beneath beholds the pangs of her dying glorious Son.

41

Quis est homo qui non fleret
Christi Matrem si videret
in tanto supplicio?

Is there one who would not
weep, whelmed in miseries
so deep Christ's dear
Mother to behold?

Quis non posset contristari
piam Matrem contemplari
dolentem cum Filio?

Can the human heart refrain
from partaking in her pain,
in that Mother's pain
untold?

Pro peccatis Suae gentis
vidit Jesum in tormentis
et flagellis subditum.

For the sins of His own
nation she saw Him hang in
desolation, all with bloody
scourges rent.

Vidit suum dulcem Natum
morientem desolatum
dum emisit spiritum.

She beheld her gentle Child
dying, forsaken and defiled,
as His spirit passed away.

(The first eight stanzas of the 'Stabat Mater')

The 'Stabat Mater dolorosa' is a hymn composed some time in the twelfth or thirteenth centuries by an unknown author (though St Bonaventure and Pope Innocent III are among those to whom it has been ascribed). In the later Middle Ages it was introduced into the liturgy, where it was regularly used on feasts of the Virgin until the 1960s. It is still used for the Stations of the Cross. There were many English translations, of which the above, by Edward Caswall (1814–78) is the best known.

The Virgin Mary is pictured at the foot of the Cross, full of grief at the torture and coming death of her son. The simple form of the poem, with each stanza consisting of three lines, with the first two rhyming, and the third line rhyming with the third line of the next stanza (aac, bbc, ddf, eef, etc.), gives an impression of a calm, mournful progression. The translation brilliantly reflects the sombre mood, and the tenderness, of the original.

Various allusions remind us of the predestined nature of her fate and that of her son. The mention, for example, of the sword finally passing through her soul, is a direct reference to Simeon's words to Mary, at the presentation of Christ in the Temple: 'Yea, a sword shall pierce through thy own soul also.' And the reference to the 'only-begotten of the Father', 'Unigenitus', reminds us not only of the divine nature of Christ, but also of the Annunciation, and the Angel Gabriel's announcement to Mary that she would give birth to the Son of God.

The poem contains a tension between on the one hand the divine nature of Christ and the 'highly blest' nature of the Virgin, and on the other the human emotions of grief that she experiences. Jesus is her 'dying *glorious* Son', the 'sole-begotten One', yet we, as humans ('Quis est homo qui non fleret'), are asked to empathize with the human emotions of a mother, and to 'partake in her pain'. The name Mary is not mentioned. She is characterized as the archetypal mother: 'the mournful Mother weeping'; 'the Mother highly blest', 'Christ's dear Mother', 'that Mother's pain'.

In a sense, this is as much a poem about human suffering as one specifically about the Virgin Mary beneath the Cross. Mary stands for all mothers who have lost their children, or seen them suffer: the mothers of Beslan, of Aberfan, of Auschwitz.

Reflections

Jesus's divinity had been announced to Mary by the angel. This had been confirmed by Simeon at the presentation of Christ in the Temple. Yet what we see, in the grieving Mary of the Stabat Mater, is a mother for whom all that matters is that her beloved son is in torment. The relationship is a human one. This is perhaps something we should think about in more depth. If Christ took on our humanity fully, in order to share our human sufferings, he must have been a normal loving son throughout his childhood and adolescence. We are told, in the Bible, next to nothing about the family life of Joseph, Mary and Jesus. We can imagine, however, that it was a close and loving family. One of the few bits of evidence we have bears this out. When the twelve-year-old Jesus stayed behind in Jerusalem, and his parents did not realize that he had done so until they were well on their return journey to Nazareth, they immediately rushed back in a panic to look for him, and when they had found him Mary, as any mother would, remonstrated with him, asking him: 'Son, why hast thou thus dealt with us? Behold, thy father and I have sought thee sorrowing.' Nothing could be more human; those of us who have been parents of young children all know the feeling, when for example they have stayed out late and we have awaited their return, full of anxiety. Then, in our relief, we can't help asking why they have put us through all this.

The closeness of the relationship is shown, too, by Jesus's care for Mary, even in the midst of his sufferings. Of the seven words from the Cross, six are entirely concerned with his mission. When he sees his mother at the foot of the Cross, however, he expresses his own concern about her situation, and entrusts her to the beloved disciple:

> Now there stood by the cross of Jesus his mother, and his mother's sister, Mary the wife of Cleophas, and Mary Magdalene.
> When Jesus therefore saw his mother, and the disciple standing by, whom he loved, he saith unto his mother, Woman, behold thy son!
> Then saith he to the disciple, Behold thy mother! And from that hour that disciple took her unto his own home.
>
> (John 19.25–27)

Mary is the saint in whom the Son of God himself became man, but she is also a human mother. The mystical view of Mary needs to be balanced by the human one. The human and the divine are intermingled in the story of the Passion, and are equally intermingled in the nature of Mary. Mary, as depicted at the Passion, is the epitome of motherly love, and Jesus shows filial love towards her when he entrusts her to the beloved disciple. This human story is paralleled by the divine story of God's love for the world: 'God so loved the world that he gave his only-begotten Son.' Human love is a reflection of God's love.

It is difficult for a man to talk about a mother's love and suffering. We can only see it from outside, but we can still wonder at its all-embracing nature. Most of us, for example, have witnessed a mother's overwhelming grief for a child that has died before its time. We can also marvel at a mother's sorrowful but all-embracing love for a child who will never be like others. Above all, we can witness to a mother's never-failing forgiveness for an adult child who has gone astray, or who has turned against her. This is a love that repays ingratitude with caring; this is a love that never fails; this is a love that can let go, at enormous personal cost – just as God lets us go, in his infinite love, to make our own way.

It is no surprise to find that God's love for humanity is, in the Old Testament, equated to a mother's love for her child. 'As one whom his mother comforteth, so will I comfort you' (Isaiah 66.13). This highest form of human love (which is closely involved in suffering, from the suffering of child-birth onwards) is thus seen as the best way of describing the nature of God's love. And just as a good mother is always prepared to forgive her child, whatever he or she has done, so God is perpetually open to us, and to our repentance. And he rejoices over the one lost sheep, the one lost coin, which is more valuable than all the others that have not been lost.

So, through the experience of human love, we can become aware of the nature of God's love for us; and human and divine love are two sides of the same coin. The nineteenth-century Dominican Henri Lacordaire once said that 'There are not two loves.' If human love is in fact a reflection of divine love, the experience of loving another human being can bring us closer to understanding God.

Not all of us can be mothers; but as we think about this mystery, it is worth assessing the extent to which our human love for our fellow-beings lives up to the sacrificial, suffering love of Jesus for all humankind – that love which is reflected in the suffering love of Mary, and of all true mothers.

Good Friday 3

'My God, my God'

One asks oneself why he let out that terrible cry.
All the texts are formal on the point, he uttered at that
    moment a terrible cry.
One asks oneself why, at that moment, he uttered such
    a terrible cry.
It should have been the opposite. He should have been
    glad.
It was finished.
It was done.
Everything had been consummated.
His passion was over; his incarnation was to all
    intents and purposes over; his passion had been
    consummated; done; redemption had been
    accomplished. Done.
All that was left was that formality (for him) of death.
Redemption had been accomplished and crowned;
Crowned with thorns, the supreme crown.
It is at that moment that he should have, ought to have,
    been happy. [. . .]

As he was about to re-enter his eternity,
On the point of re-entering his eternity,
It was then, all the texts are in agreement, the texts are
formal on the point, it was then that he uttered that
dreadful cry. [. . .]

A cry that still resounds through all humanity;
A cry that made the Church militant totter on its
foundations;
A cry in which suffering experienced its own terror;
A cry as though God himself had sinned like us;
As though even God had felt despair;
A cry as though God had sinned like us;
With the greatest sin.
Which is to despair.

The sin of despair.

More than the two thieves hanging at his side;
Howling at death like skinny dogs.
The thieves were merely howling with a human howl;
The thieves were merely howling with a cry of human
death;
They were merely slobbering with human slobber:

The Just alone uttered the eternal cry.

But why? What was wrong with him?

(Charles Péguy, Extract from *Le Mystère de la charité de Jeanne d'Arc*)

Charles Péguy (1873–1914) was born in Orleans of peasant stock, but was educated in Paris at the Ecole Normale Supérieure, and became a fervent socialist and a journalist. Around 1908 he refound his faith as a Catholic Christian, and in 1910 published his *Mystère de la charité de Jeanne d'Arc*, a long poem of which the centrepiece is the vivid and moving description of Christ's Passion. Péguy is a most unusual poet, who uses the techniques of ordinary speech, the repetitions, the banalities, in order to give a realistic picture of simple minds struggling to grasp complex problems.

Jesus's cry, 'My God, my God, why hast thou forsaken me?' is one of the most shocking moments in the whole story of the Crucifixion. Here is Jesus, the Son of God, apparently in despair, crying out that God has forsaken him. It seems, at first, as though the whole story of the Crucifixion, and its meaning, have been undermined.

At first sight, this extract from Péguy's *Mystery of the Charity of Joan of Arc* may seem off-putting in its repetitions, its apparent banality, its unpoetic language, all of which are typical of Péguy. It is part of a long passage in which a companion of Joan of Arc's, a simple peasant woman, is meditating on the Passion. Péguy's style is here particularly suitable, as it conveys the picture of a simple woman asking a simple question.

It is Jesus's cry, described as 'a cry which rang false, like a divine blasphemy', that causes her the greatest problem. If Jesus Christ was God, if the Crucifixion was the climax of his mission, why is there this moment of apparent doubt and despair?

As if she needs to be clear that it actually took place, she stresses the authorities for this account of Christ's words:

'All the texts are formal on the point'; 'All the texts are in agreement, the texts are formal on the point.' Yet she cannot understand why it should have happened. He should have been happy, not despairing. Echoing the words 'It is finished', 'Consummatum est', she describes how he had fulfilled his mission. Note, again, the use of the banality of the clichés of everyday speech, so out of proportion with the great events that are being described (his Incarnation was '*to all intents and purposes* over'), and the repetition of the stark word 'done', to denote that his mission had been fulfilled. Even the punctuation, disjointing as it does the message, accentuates the conversational tone. And the necessity of Christ's death is similarly described as though it were part of some official procedure: 'All that was left was the formality (for him) of death.'

Hidden within these banal forms of expression, however, are ultimate truths. 'Redemption had been accomplished and crowned', and, because that redemption was achieved through suffering, its crown was a crown of thorns, 'the supreme crown'. And, to her simple mind, that was the moment that 'he should have, ought to have, been happy.' (Note, again, the repetitions, as in ordinary speech, trying to get the right word.) It was the moment when Christ, the Word, was departing mortal life and 're-entering his eternity'. Why, then, at this moment, did he utter 'that dreadful cry'?

She then proceeds to expand on the effect of that cry on all those who hear of it. It still resounds, and it appears to undermine all the teachings of the Church, because it is as though *God* was suffering, was terrified, as though God was in despair. And despair is described as a sin, the greatest sin of them all. So God was apparently sinning like humankind. Again, the punctuation, with short phrases serving as sentences divided by full stops, accentuates the nature of despair.

Finally, she compares the cries of the thieves crucified alongside him with his cry, which is 'eternal'. And she ends up with the simple question, couched in simple, everyday language: 'But why? What was wrong with him?'

We are, of course, left with the same question: what was wrong with him? Why should God, Jesus, have emitted such a cry of despair? And there is no denying, despite the fact that this is a quotation from Psalm 22 (which has given rise to all kinds of theological interpretations of its meaning), that Jesus is here clearly in real despair. Péguy is right in describing it as 'a terrible cry', 'a dreadful cry'.

Joan's companion, however, by stressing solely the divinity of Christ, has surely missed part of the meaning of all this. She thinks, how can this be? Christ is God. He knows that he will rise again, he knows that he is on the point of accomplishing his divine mission, and that all his suffering is part of the divine purpose. So, to repeat her question: 'Why? What was wrong with him?'

Reflections

This moment in the Crucifixion is something which gives us greater insight into the mystery of the Incarnation. It is probably wrong to start, like the speaker in the poem, from Jesus as God. The mystery of the Incarnation is that Jesus is both God and man. He, who has been part of God from the beginning of time, has taken on the body of a man, in order to share fully in our experiences, and to be the mediator between God and man. He has come to save us from our sins, by suffering on our behalf. It is through his suffering that we are saved. This mystery is explained in the Epistle to the Hebrews:

51

Since all children share the same human nature, he too shared equally in it, so that by his death he could set aside him who held the power of death, namely the devil, and set free all those who had been held in slavery all their lives by the fear of death;

For it was not the angels that he took to himself; he took to himself the line of Abraham.

It was essential that he should in this way be made completely like his brothers, so that he could become a compassionate and trustworthy high priest for their relationship to God, able to expiate the sins of the people.

For the suffering he himself passed through while being put to the test enables him to help others when they are being put to the test.

(Hebrews 2.14–18)

So Jesus, as a man, must suffer really, in the flesh. He has set aside his divinity for this supreme test. That suffering would not mean much unless it was really felt, in the way that we humans feel suffering. It is as a man that Jesus is suffering there on the Cross. Only in this way can he fully share in the nature of humanity.

One of the greatest forms of suffering is mental suffering. Mental anguish can be caused by a variety of causes: mental illness, physical suffering, harrowing events in one's life, fear. Some people manage to get through life without such anguish. Most of us don't. And yet such suffering is only too often discounted by those around the sufferer. Where sympathy can be felt for someone who has a physical ailment, there is a tendency to be impatient with mental sufferers, to feel that they really ought to 'pull themselves together' – and sometimes even to tell them so.

When Jesus took on our humanity, he took it on completely. He was prepared to undergo even our worst experiences – fear, anguish, despair. Thus, before the Crucifixion, we find him flinching at the thought of the suffering that awaited him. That fear surfaced when he prayed to God the Father that 'this cup' of suffering should be removed from him, and that he should not have to go through with it. The gospel tells us that he was in such agony that 'his sweat was as it were great drops of blood falling down on the ground.' George Herbert, in his great poem 'The Agony', graphically depicts that scene, while stressing that it is 'a man' who is suffering it all:

> Who would know Sin, let him repair
> Unto Mount Olivet; there shall he see
> A man so wrung with pain, that all his hair,
>   His skin, his garments bloody be.
> Sin is that press and vice, which forceth pain
> To hunt his cruel food through ev'ry vein.

Jesus had to be *seen* to suffer as we suffer. He had to suffer both physically and mentally. He had to show that he was there for us all.

Péguy, and Herbert, both seem to suggest, in the poems we have read, that despair is a sin, 'the greatest sin'. Christ's own despair surely shows us, however, that though despair *is* a purely human attribute, he in his humanity can share even in that, and that our despair and doubt are understood rather than condemned by him.

In Jesus's cry of despair, 'My God, my God, why hast thou forsaken me?', we find not only the expression of that human suffering experience, but also a preparation for the acceptance, and understanding, that Jesus will show in his final words, 'It is finished', 'It is completed', 'My mission is done.' For his mission would not have been fulfilled, unless he had plumbed the profoundest depths of human suffering, mental and physical. And in his suffering we can find some consolation for our own.

Good Friday 4

The good thief

You did not see Him on the mountain of Transfiguration
    Nor walking the sea at night;
You never saw corpses blushing when a bier or sepulchre
    Was struck by his cry.

It was in the rawness of his flesh and his dirt that you
    saw Him,
    Whipped and under thorns,
And in his nailing like a sack of bones outside the town
    On a pole, like a scarecrow.

You never heard the making of parables like a
    Parthenon of words,
    Nor his tone when He talked of His Father,
Neither did you hear the secrets of the room above,
    Nor the prayer before Cedron and the treachery.

It was in the racket of a crowd of sadists revelling in
    pain
    And their screeches, howls, curses and shouts
That you heard the profound cry of the breaking heart
    of their prey:
    'Why hast thou forsaken me?'

You, hanging on his right; on his left, your brother;
   Writhing like skinned frogs,
Flea-bitten petty thieves thrown in as a retinue to his
   shame,
   Courtiers to a mock king in his pain.

O master of courtesy and manners, who enlightened
   you
   About your part in this harsh parody?
'Lord, when you come into your kingdom, remember
   me,' –
   The kingdom that was conquered through death.

Rex Judaeorum; it was you who saw first the vain
   Blasphemy as a living oracle,
You who first believed in the Latin, Hebrew and Greek,
   That the gallows was the throne of God.

O thief who took Paradise from the nails of a gibbet,
   Foremost of the nobilitas of heaven,
Before the hour of death pray that it may be given to
   us
   To perceive Him and to taste Him.

(Saunders Lewis, 'To the Good Thief' ('I'r Lleidr Da', translated by
Gwyn Thomas))

Saunders Lewis (1893–1985), one of the founders of the Welsh Nationalist Party, Plaid Cymru, was born in Wallasey, Cheshire. His family were prominent Calvinistic Methodists, his father and grandfather being ministers. Strongly influenced by the French authors of the Catholic Right, he was received into the Roman Catholic Church in 1932. By many, he is considered to be the greatest figure in twentieth-century Welsh literature, as dramatist, essayist and poet. His poetic output was small, but includes some fine religious poems, of which this is an example.

Péguy described the two thieves hanging at Jesus's side as 'howling at death like skinny dogs . . . howling with a human howl, with a cry of human death'. Yet this is too simple a description of them. Admittedly, in the gospels of St Matthew and St Mark, the thieves are shown merely as joining in the mockery of Jesus; but Luke was to give a very different story, in which one of the thieves showed spiritual insight of a rare kind, and thereby inspired one of Jesus's most telling statements from the Cross:

> And one of the malefactors which were hanged railed on him, saying, If thou be the Christ, save thyself and us.
> But the other answering rebuked him, saying, Dost not thou fear God, seeing thou art in the same condemnation?
> And we indeed justly; for we receive the due reward of our deeds: but this man hath done nothing amiss.
> And he said unto Jesus, Lord, remember me when thou comest into thy kingdom.

And Jesus said unto him, Verily I say unto thee, Today shalt thou be with me in paradise.

(Luke 23.39–43)

In his poem, Saunders Lewis muses on this scene. As in Péguy's description, the two thieves are 'writhing like skinned frogs'. Lewis expresses wonderment, however, at the insight shown by the good thief. In the first two stanzas he contrasts the experience of Jesus's disciples with that of this petty criminal. Peter and the others had seen the Transfiguration, had seen Jesus walking on the water, had seen him raising Lazarus from the dead. All the thief has seen is a man physically suffering on the Cross, in abject filth and tortured flesh, 'a sack of bones . . . on a pole, like a scarecrow'. In stanzas 3 and 4 we again have the contrast between the thief and the disciples, this time in relation to what they had heard from Jesus. The disciples had been taught by his parables, they had heard him speak of God his Father, they had been taught by him in the upper room before his arrest, they had heard his prayer before his Passion, in which, despite his human fears, he had accepted God's decision as to his fate. All the thief had heard from him was the desolate cry, 'My God, my God . . .' as he was surrounded by the shouts and mockery of the crowd; the cry that seemed to say that even Jesus momentarily doubted of his mission.

Yet this man has shown more insight than the disciples ever had. Even when Jesus told his disciples what was going to happen to him, the gospel tells us that they did not understand what he said. At the time of his arrest they fell into a disarray that reveals how little they had understood of what they had heard. Most of them fled; Simon Peter denied him three times, through fear; and even after Jesus's death, they seem to have been unaware, until events revealed it to them, that Jesus (who had told them what to expect) was to rise from the dead. As the disciples walked to Emmaus they recounted, with downcast faces, 'how the chief priests and our rulers delivered him to be condemned to death, and have crucified him', and sighed, 'but we trusted that it had been he which should have redeemed Israel' (Luke 24.20–21).

What the disciples failed to see, this thief perceives clearly, without having been given any of the evidence. As Lewis says, 'Who enlightened you?' We are to take it that God has vouchsafed this insight to him (in the way that Jesus described God as having inspired the ignorant fisherman Peter, when he confessed at Caesarea Philippi that Jesus was the Christ: 'Blessed art thou, Simon Bar-jona: for flesh and blood hath not revealed it unto thee, but my Father which is in heaven', Matthew 16.17). It is this insight which first of all leads the good thief to contradict his companion's mockery of Jesus, telling him that 'this man hath done nothing amiss.' He then cuts across other people's mockery of Christ's kingship, and is the only person who at this point takes seriously the title that is written above Jesus's head, 'in letters of Greek, and Latin, and Hebrew, THIS IS THE KING OF THE JEWS'. 'Remember me when you come into your kingdom,' he says. As Lewis puts it: '*Rex Judaeorum*: it was you who saw first the vain blasphemy as a living oracle, you who first believed in the Latin, Hebrew and Greek, that the gallows was the throne of God.'

What the thief has seen is that Jesus's kingdom is 'not of this world'. The disciples, despite Jesus's teaching, had continued to expect that 'he would be the one to set Israel free', and had therefore been completely thrown by his arrest and Crucifixion. Immediately after one of the occasions when Jesus had told them that he would be delivered into the hands of the chief priests and the scribes, and would be condemned to death, James and John had asked him (as though they hadn't even heard what he said) to grant that they should sit, one on his right hand and the other on his left, when he came into his glory. How ironic that those who were eventually at his right hand and his left, as his mission was fulfilled, should be two miserable thieves! And that one of them should have been vouchsafed a promise far greater that what James and John had asked for: 'Today shalt thou be with me in paradise.'

So that thief is now 'foremost in the nobilitas of heaven'. The precedence of this earth has been reversed. Jesus, who socialized with tax collectors and prostitutes, and with other people whom the Jews believed to be sinful, sees the good in all, even the most apparently sinful and abject. No sinner can be too awful to be refused forgiveness, and a whole series of Jesus's parables showed that a repentant sinner was a cause of greater joy than all those who had never strayed. Now, on the Cross, Jesus once more reinforces that message.

The words 'before the hour of death, pray' are a conscious reminder of the Angelus, when we ask the Virgin Mary to 'pray for us sinners, now and at the hour of our death.' Lewis, the Catholic, has declared the good thief, because he was the first to witness to the divinity of the dying Christ, to be 'foremost among the nobilitas of heaven'. So Lewis finally asks him, as a saint, to pray on our behalf, to pray that we, before we die, may be granted the same insight as he has had; that we may perceive Jesus Christ clearly for what he is, and that we may taste the experience of his presence.

Jesus, as we saw when considering his cry 'My God, my God, why hast thou forsaken me', was undertaking suffering on the Cross as a human being. It is hardly surprising that those who saw him hanging there should have discounted his claim to kingship. How could a king, how could the Son of God, be submitted to such ignominy? Where was God? Why did he not intervene, if this was his son?

Yet God moves in a mysterious way, and his justice is not like our human justice. Jesus's mission was to suffer; this was God's way of saving humankind. But those who observed the scene on the Cross did not know this. Alongside all those who saw, in Christ's suffering, the disproof of his divine claims, there was, however, one person who saw clearly what Jesus was.

Why was this insight given to a petty thief, and denied to 'the great and the good'? Is there something we can learn from it? Perhaps there is a message over and above the one that everyone in this world, even the greatest sinners, can be recipients of God's grace. That further message is that we, too, need to cultivate insight, to learn to see through the outside appearances into the inner truth of other people's lives. It is so easy to jump to conclusions about people, so easy to be intolerant of what we believe to be error, so easy to react badly to the way other people behave, without attempting to work out the reasons for their behaviour.

If it was difficult for Christ's contemporaries to have insight into who he was, it is difficult for us, in our own time, to have insight into the true being of those around us. All we know is that our paradoxical God hides good within the appearances of evil, gentleness within rough exteriors, unselfishness within shells of selfishness.

It is hard to have insight into the designs of God. It is hard to have insight into those around us. But perhaps the hardest thing of all is to have insight into ourselves.

Easter Eve

Doubt and uncertainty, faith and trust

Awhile meet Doubt and Faith:
   For either sigheth and saith,
   That He is dead,
   To-day: the linen cloths cover His head,
That hath, at last, whereon to rest; a rocky bed.

Come! For the pangs are done,
   That overcast the sun,
   So bright to-day!
   And moved the Roman soldier: come away!
Hath sorrow more to weep? Hath pity more to say?

Why wilt thou linger yet?
   Think on dark Olivet;
   On Calvary stem:
   Think, from the happy birth at Bethlehem,
To this last woe and passion at Jerusalem!

This only can be said:
   He loved us all; is dead;
   May rise again.
   But if He rise not? Over the far main,
The sun of glory falls indeed: the stars are plain.

(Lionel Johnson, 'A Burden of Easter Vigil')

Lionel Johnson (1867–1902), educated at Winchester and New College, Oxford, was a prominent convert to Roman Catholicism, being received into the Church in 1891. He published two collections of verse, *Poems* (1895) and *Ireland and other poems* (1897). A serious drink problem led to his early death at the age of 35. At its best, his poetry is a subtle and at times tortured testimony to his profound Christian faith.

We seldom think of what it must have been like for the disciples the day after the Crucifixion. The disarray into which they had fallen at the time of Jesus's arrest and execution must have continued, only to be dispelled on Easter Day with the revelation of his Resurrection. For the time being, the future was in doubt. Accounts suggest that they had no inkling of the momentous things that were about to happen. Even if they *had* partly taken on board the teachings that Jesus had given them about his death and Resurrection, immediately after the Crucifixion there must have been uncertainty as to whether anything of the kind would take place. That mood is brilliantly caught in this poem.

Much of its disturbing effect is created by the voice that is used, and the complex viewpoint from which the poem is being written. From the second stanza onwards (their situation having been described in general terms in the first stanza), a voice addresses the disciples directly. But who is this speaker? The voice speaking in the poem is clearly separate from the grieving disciples whom it is addressing. On the other hand, that voice itself shares in a number of the attitudes of the disciples in the period before the Resurrection, and appears to be contemporary with them;

it must therefore be distinguished from the poet, Johnson, who is creating it, and who *knows* that the Resurrection was about to take place. This complexity provides a tension which, by the final stanza, is almost unbearable.

The verse-form in which the poem is written adds, at times, to the impact of what is being said, with the short central line being used to great effect. We start with the juxtaposition of the two apparently contradictory words, 'Doubt' and 'Faith', concepts which are, however, intertwined in most Christian experience, and are here clearly described as both being present in the minds of the disciples. Johnson suggests that doubt and faith agree on one point: their sadness, as they contemplate the fact that Christ is dead (with the words 'that He is dead / to-day' starkly stated in the shortest line of the stanza, and with the enjambement – the carrying-over of a section of a phrase into the next line – dramatically singling out one word of the sentence, 'to-day', and stressing the apparent finality of the situation, and also that it is here and now that it has happened). The evocation of the linen cloths that cover his head not only further stresses the fact of death, but also, to the reader who (unlike the disciples) is certain that the Resurrection is going to happen on the next morning, suggests one of the salient points of the Resurrection story. Thus we already have a kind of complicity between the poet and us, the readers, all of whom are aware of things that the disciples who are being described, and the person who is speaking to them, cannot know.

This first stanza is particularly rich in allusions. The final phrase in it echoes Christ's saying: 'Foxes have holes, and birds of the air have nests, but the Son of Man has nowhere to lay his head.' Only in death has Jesus found a place to rest his head; a stone slab.

The ambiguous voice we have described now calls on the disciples, in exclamatory tone ('Come! ... Come away!'), to give up weeping and pity; Christ's pains are over. The sun had been overcast, and 'darkness had been over the land' from the sixth hour to the ninth hour, when Christ had died. But the sun is shining once more (note, again, how the short line is used to point the contrast, with the word 'to-day' once more stressing the immediacy of what is being described). Christ's pains had moved even the Roman soldier, who had exclaimed 'Truly this man was the Son of God' (Mark 15.39). But now there is no more to be said, and pity is out of place: Jesus is dead, and no weeping can alter that.

Note that the stress, here, is not on the triumph of the Cross, not on the Atonement. Jesus has suffered, and his suffering is over, and there is no point in dwelling on what has happened.

This point is further developed in the third stanza. The voice asks why the disciples are lingering in grief, thinking of the agony on the mount of Olives, and of the suffering on the Cross. (The short central line, 'On Calvary stem', starkly evokes the trunk of the Cross.) Why are they still thinking of the past, of what has happened between the joy of the Nativity and the sorrow of the Passion?

In the final stanza, the equivocal message of the voice that is speaking to us is brought out even more vividly. In a very matter-of-fact tone, it sets out the facts, in clipped, short phrases separated by colons and semicolons: 'This only can be said: he loved us all; is dead.' And then the middle line appears to change the tone: 'May rise again'. But note the mood of the verb: '*May* rise again'. The uncertainty of the 'may' is then compounded by the stark horror of the following phrase (italicized by the poet): '*But if He rise not?*'

The person whose voice speaks in the poem is as much in disarray as the disciples he or she has been addressing. Faith has been superseded by doubt. The Resurrection is uncertain. The certainties with which the facts of death have been described have been succeeded by doubt about what goes beyond what 'only can be said'. What if Christ were not to rise? 'The sun of glory falls indeed', and all that is left is the stars of the night sky.

Reflections

In this remarkable poem, Lionel Johnson has caught the despair of doubt. The faith of most Christians is similarly assailed from time to time by doubt; and, indeed, faith could neither exist nor be of any importance if an element of doubt did not enter into it. Yet it is only too easy, when assailed by doubt, to descend into despair. Johnson, in this poem, by describing such a mood of doubt in the very disciples who were within 24 hours to be galvanized by hope, has enabled us all to place our doubts into perspective, and be reassured. This is because we know that after the events of the Resurrection and of Pentecost, those doubting disciples, who had fled in terror at the time of Jesus's arrest, and who remained fearful and in uncertainty thereafter, were to become staunch witnesses to the faith, and heroic in their steadfastness throughout persecution. It took the experience of the Resurrection to produce in them the confidence to become rocks of strength. Similarly, only after being tested are we likely to come to any lasting certainty.

The phrase 'the experience of the Resurrection' is a misleading one. The disciples did not witness the Resurrection itself; they merely witnessed its after-effects. Here, again, certainties were avoided, and faith was still necessary. In another poem on Easter Eve, Johnson's fellow-convert Alice Meynell speaks of the privacy of the Resurrection.

All night had shout of men and cry
   Of woeful women filled his way;
Until that noon of sombre sky
   On Friday, clamour and display
Smote him; no solitude had he,
No silence, since Gethsemane.

Public was Death; but Power, but Might,
   But Life again, but Victory,
Were hushed within the dead of night,
   The shuttered dark, the secrecy.
And all alone, alone, alone,
He rose again behind the stone.

(Alice Meynell, 'Easter Night')

Alice Meynell (1847–1922) was converted to Roman Catholicism in 1868. She and her husband Wilfrid Meynell discovered and protected the poet Francis Thompson, and were the centre of a wide Catholic literary circle. She published several volumes of verse between 1893 and 1923, many of her poems expressing a subtle yet profound sense of religious mystery.

Unlike Johnson's poem, this is a calm evocation of certainty; and it shows us that, though the news of the Resurrection was to lead to the stirring events of the spread of the gospel, the amazing thing is that, unlike the public events of the

Crucifixion, the Resurrection only became public once it had happened, and the event itself was hidden from gaze.

This is completely unlike most of the ecstatic poems and hymns that have been written to celebrate Easter Day. Instead, it is a calm evocation of peace and quiet. Jesus had gone through all those public events, throughout Good Friday. His last moment of peace had been in the Garden of Gethsemane. His ignominious death had been public; his triumph over death, his victory, was to be private, and hidden; not in the harsh daylight, but at night, behind the stone that had been rolled in front of the tomb. Christ's solitude, even in this moment of triumph, is powerfully evoked by the triple repetition of the word 'alone'.

Reflections

Why did Christ, after his public death, rise from the dead without anyone to observe him? If the Resurrection had been public, and had been able to be described in matter-of-fact terms similar to those in which Johnson described the Crucifixion ('This only can be said: he loved us all; is dead'), there would have been no need for faith. The aftermath of the Resurrection supplies us with enough evidence for us to be able, with faith, to believe in the Resurrection itself. If everything was given to us as certainty, this faith would have been valueless. It was the virtue of the disciples that, after all the uncertainties depicted in the gospels, after all the doubts evoked by Johnson, they were able, on Easter Day and thereafter, to come to certainty through faith, and to act upon it. 'Awhile meet Faith and Doubt'; both can be present in us all.

Easter Day

The joy of Resurrection

Alleluia! Alleluia! Alleluia!
The strife is o'er, the battle done;
Now is the Victor's triumph won;
O let the song of praise be sung.
                    Alleluia!

Death's mightiest powers have done their worst,
And Jesus hath his power dispersed;
Let shouts of praise and joy outburst.
                    Alleluia!

On the third morn He rose again
Glorious in majesty to reign;
O let us swell the joyful strain.
                    Alleluia!

Lord, by the stripes which wounded Thee
From death's dread sting Thy servants free,
That we may live, and sing to Thee
                    Alleluia!

(Latin hymn of the seventeenth century, translated by Francis Pott
(1832–1909))

While much good poetry has been written on Christ's
suffering on the Cross, and on all the events leading up to
Easter, comparatively little has been produced in relation
to Easter itself. What there is tends to be in the form of
simple and straightforward expressions of joy, such as this,
which evoke Christ's victory over death and sin, and the joy

of all Christians. One approach to Easter could be just to immerse ourselves in them, and share their joy.

In 'The strife is o'er', the shouts of 'Alleluia!' which are found in the Easter liturgies dominate the whole hymn, giving a sense of exultation. This is accentuated by the insistent rhythm of the sequences of three lines, each set of three containing one rhyme only. It is as though we are being carried along by a juggernaut of joy.

The hymn starts, however, on an ambiguous note. The triumphalist imagery is couched in words which convey a worldly victory, the kind of messianic victory which those who cried 'Hosanna!' at Christ's entry into Jerusalem on Palm Sunday had envisaged as the outcome of Jesus's mission. The first stanza of 'The strife is o'er' is typical of a number of other Easter hymns in its use of military imagery to describe Christ's victory. It has been a 'battle', and the victor is entitled, like a Roman general, to a triumph (a great procession at which he is acclaimed by the people, as he leads those he has conquered, in chains). The image of the 'triumph' is then elaborated on, with us, the people, being exhorted to sing a song of praise. That song, 'Alleluia!', immediately follows this.

Though the same imagery permeates the second stanza, it is now clear that the opponent has nothing to do with a worldly victory. The opponent is Death, here personified. Christ has 'dispersed' his enemies, and once again we are exhorted to let out shouts of praise and joy, and the cry of 'Alleluia!' returns.

The last two stanzas bring us the true message of Easter. In the first of these the events of Easter morning are invoked. Christ has risen; Christ will reign in glory. And again the exhortation follows, to sing of joy. The final stanza relates this to ourselves. We pray, by Jesus's wounds, by his suffering that has redeemed us, that he will free us from death, as is promised by his Resurrection. Christ's victory has been achieved by his suffering. His victory over death is the victory of the suffering God. His kingdom is not of this world.

This is a powerful and effective piece of poetry, which conveys the joy of the Day of Resurrection. It has an immediate and simple appeal. There are a few poems which go beyond this, however, on the subject of Easter. If we want further scope for meditation, there are a number of poems by George Herbert (1593–1633) and Henry Vaughan (1621–95), which provide us with richer veins of thought. One of the best, by Henry Vaughan, is entitled simply 'Easter-day'.

> Thou, whose sad heart and weeping head lies low,
>   Whose cloudy breast cold damps invade,
> Who never feel'st the Sun, nor smooth'st thy brow,
>   But sitt'st oppressèd in the shade,
>   Awake, awake,
> And in his Resurrection partake,
>   Who on this day (that thou might'st rise as he)
>   Rose up, and cancelled two deaths due to thee.
>
> Awake, awake; and like the Sun, disperse
>   All mists that would usurp this day;
> Where are thy palms, thy branches, and thy verse?
>   *Hosanna!* hark, why dost thou stay?
>   Arise, arise,
> And with his healing blood anoint thine eyes,
>   Thy inward eyes; his blood will cure thy mind,
>   Whose spittle only could restore the blind.

(Henry Vaughan, 'Easter-day')

Henry Vaughan (1621–95), known as 'the Silurist', was the son of a Welsh gentleman of Newton-upon-Usk, Breconshire. After leaving Jesus College, Oxford, without a degree, he studied law, and later medicine, practising as a doctor in his native county. He was a Royalist (fighting on the King's side in the Civil War), and a devout member of the Church of England. His early secular poetry is weak, but with a collection entitled *Silex Scintillans* (1650) he emerged as a major religious poet, whose poems often have a pronounced mystical quality, enhanced by subtle references to detail of the biblical text.

Vaughan was a great admirer of his predecessor George Herbert (1593–1633), and this poem is based on one of Herbert's, also about Easter, entitled 'The Dawning'. Vaughan's poem is infinitely superior, however, in that, though Herbert evoked well the change in heart brought about in the disciples after they came to the tomb 'towards dawn' (Matthew 28.1), his poem (which had exactly the same shape as Vaughan's) was spoilt by an over-precious conceit (or elaborate metaphor comparing apparently dissimilar objects in a surprising way) in the final lines:

> Arise, arise,
> And with his burial-linen dry your eyes:
>   Christ left his grave-clothes, that we might, when grief
>   Draws tears, or blood, not want a handkerchief.

(George Herbert, 'The Dawning')

Vaughan, while using what was best in Herbert's poem (the urgent call, in the short line in each stanza, to 'Awake, awake', 'Arise, arise'), and while adding further urgency by repeating 'Awake, awake' at the beginning of the second stanza, fills out the rest of the poem with a series of allusions which force us to think about the real meaning of what has happened.

In the first stanza we have a clarion call to put aside melancholy and 'partake' (share) in Christ's Resurrection. In other words, we are not merely to rejoice in it from outside (as in so many Easter hymns), but to make it part of our own experience. This idea of 'partaking' in Christ's Resurrection stems from the passage in the book of Revelation (20.6): 'Blessed and holy is he that hath part in the first resurrection; on such the second death hath no power.' When Christ rose, he conquered death on our behalf. He 'cancelled two deaths'; the temporal death at the end of our lives, in that we now through Christ's Resurrection have the promise of life eternal; and the spiritual death, the 'second death' brought about by sin, the death of the condemned soul at the Last Judgement. What Revelation tells us is that from that second death we are redeemed by Christ's suffering on our behalf, if, sharing in Christ's Resurrection, we open ourselves to the spiritual insight which is on offer to us. This theme will be enlarged upon at the end of the second stanza.

At the beginning of the second stanza, we are again called upon to awake. Why are we not rejoicing? The mention of palms and branches brings to mind the rejoicings of the people on Palm Sunday, their 'verse' ('thy palms, thy branches, and thy verse') being 'Blessed is he that comes in the name of the Lord. Hosanna in the highest!' The difference is, of course, that the people of Jerusalem had not undertood the nature of the kingship of the Messiah, and had thought that they were hailing someone who would bring about the physical deliverance of Israel; whereas we know his kingship to be based in his suffering, his offering of his blood on our behalf and his triumphant Resurrection.

This is brought out in the last three lines, in a complicated and highly successful conceit. We are spiritually blind. We must anoint our eyes (by which Vaughan explains that he means our 'spiritual eyes') with Christ's blood, which will heal our minds in the way that Christ's spittle healed the physical ills of the blind man (John 9; Mark 8).

Throughout the poem the point is being made that Christ has saved us both from physical death and from spiritual death (the death of sin), and that his redeeming blood is there to open our spiritual eyes and make us spiritually whole. It is a plea for us to wake up to these facts, and to 'partake' rather than standing back; for Christ's redemption is available to us only if we avail ourselves of it.

Reflections

Vaughan has told us, following the words of Revelation, that Christ's Resurrection, if we bring ourselves to share in it, will open our spiritual eyes, and we will no longer be blind. In other words, it is not enough merely to rejoice in the Resurrection. What is needed is a commitment on our part.

It is no coincidence that Easter Day was, in the early Church, the day of baptism for all those adult catechumens who had spent the time of Lent preparing for it by prayer and fasting. Easter morning, the culmination of that preparation, must have been a very dramatic moment, as the catechumens, who had spent the night in the church, witnessed the sunrise. It was the moment of Christ's

Resurrection, and at the same time the moment of their own resurrection into a new life in Christ. The Orthodox Church's prayer for catechumens stresses the 'light' of the new day that is dawning for them, in which they will 'know' God:

Bless, O Lord, these your catechumens whom you have called through a holy calling to the wonderful light of knowing you: help them to know the sure foundation of your word on which their instruction rests. Pour your Holy Spirit upon them that they too may become the little sheep of the one true shepherd, signed with the seal of the Holy Spirit and precious members of the body of your Church.

At Eastertime it is worth our thinking ourselves into the situation of those catechumens. Most of us have been baptized, and confirmed; but in most of us the imprint of that baptism and confirmation has dimmed. It is for this reason that, in the Service of Light in the Easter Vigil, we take once more our baptismal vows in a solemn ceremony in which the imagery of light is central, and in which we pray that God may 'set us aflame with the fire of your love, and bring us to the radiance of your glory.' The priest's exhortation to the congregation to retake their vows contains the imagery of death and resurrection:

As we celebrate the resurrection of our Lord Jesus Christ from the dead, we remember that through the paschal mystery we have died and been buried with him in baptism, so that we may rise with him to a new life within the family of his Church. Now that we have completed our observance of Lent, we renew the promises made at our baptism, affirming our allegiance to Christ, and our rejection of all that is evil.

This echoes Vaughan's exhortation to 'share' in the Resurrection of Christ. Just as Christians are called not to stand by like the onlookers at the Crucifixion of Jesus, but to participate in it, so they are called not just to rejoice in the Resurrection, but to be resurrected themselves, renewing their 'life within the family of the Church'.

A lot of the Easter message has to do with sight, with recognition. Have you noticed how difficult the disciples found it, to recognize the risen Jesus? In St John's Gospel account, Mary Magdalene meets Jesus by the tomb. But she does not recognize him. She presumes he is the gardener, and says to him, 'Sir, if thou borne him hence, tell me where thou hast laid him, and I will take him away.' It is only when Jesus says her name that she recognizes him. All he has to say is the one word, 'Mary', and she responds with the one word, 'Master' (John 20).

Similarly, in St Luke's Gospel (Chapter 24) we find two of the disciples walking to Emmaus. They are joined by a stranger, whom they do not recognize. They tell him all that has been going on, showing the disarray in which they are, like the other disciples – the despondency into which they have fallen through what has seemed the dashing of all their hopes. The stranger teaches them, through the scriptures, the true meaning of all that has happened. But it is only when they sit down to supper together, and he breaks and blesses the bread, that they realize that this is Jesus.

In other words, their 'inward eyes' were cured. Like them, we are given the opportunity, at Easter, to perceive clearly the person of the risen Jesus. The gift of Easter, for all of us, is that of sight, of insight. If we 'partake' in the experience of the Resurrection, we can begin to see Jesus clearly in all around us. We can perceive, within other human beings, the element of the godlike. And, above all, we can see Jesus in all the poor and the suffering with whom he has identified himself, and through whom we can become worthy of him. 'For I was an hungred, and ye gave me meat: I was thirsty, and ye gave me drink: I was a stranger, and ye took me in: Naked, and ye clothed me: I was sick, and ye visited me: I was in prison, and ye came unto me' (Matthew 25.35–36). When Jesus calls us by name, as he called Mary; when Jesus's body, the bread on the altar, is broken in our presence, as he broke the bread for the disciples at Emmaus; then we too can be spiritually cured, and see clearly.

CHAPTER FOUR

Three Meditations for Christmastide

Advent

Creator and created

No sudden thing of glory and fear
Was the Lord's coming; but the dear
  Slow Nature's days followed each other
  To form the Saviour from His Mother
– One of the children of the year.

The earth, the rain, received the trust,
– The sun and dews, to frame the Just.
  He drew His daily life from these,
  According to His own decrees
Who makes man from the fertile dust.

Sweet summer and the winter wild,
These brought Him forth, the Undefiled.
  The happy Spring renewed again
  His daily bread, the growing grain,
The food and raiment of the Child.

(Alice Meynell, 'Advent Meditation')[12]

Alice Meynell's poetry is always deceptively simple. Each poem usually deals, shortly and clearly, with one profound idea; but we, the readers, are led into areas of thought which go far beyond the apparent simplicity of that idea. In this poem, about the time of waiting for the Incarnation of Jesus, the central idea is the paradox whereby God, the Creator of the universe, is about to create a baby who is himself. In other words, he is both the Creator and the created.

In the first stanza, the contrast is drawn between the coming of the Messiah, as visualized by the people of Israel, and what actually happened. Those expecting the Messiah must have visualized him coming in glory, like the figure in Psalm 24:

Lift up your heads, O ye gates; and be ye lift up, ye everlasting doors; and the King of glory shall come in. Who is this King of glory? The Lord strong and mighty, the Lord mighty in battle. Lift up your heads, O ye gates; even lift them up, ye everlasting doors; and the King of glory shall come in. Who is this King of glory? The Lord of hosts, he is the King of glory.

(Psalm 24.7–10)

12. For a short note on Alice Meynell, see p. 66.

But Christ was not destined to come 'in glory'; nor would he come instilling 'fear'. He was to come into the world just like every other baby, formed gradually during his mother's pregnancy. How telling, to mothers listening to this poem, must the phrase describing the slow, burdensome waiting be! 'Slow Nature's days followed each other.' And this natural process was just like that undergone by all the other mothers, and all the other 'children of the year'.

The second stanza now shows how his infancy was to be just like any other. He drew his daily life from the nature around him. But suddenly, in the last two lines of the stanza, the central paradox of the poem is revealed. It is he who has created the natural laws under which he now exists. He created man from dust, and now he himself has been created.

The final stanza enlarges on this, showing how the seasons catered for him. He was carried by his mother through the autumn, and he was born in winter. Then, in the spring, he started life, with the same needs as another child: 'his daily bread', which spring created alongside him, in the growing grain. The references to his divine status are not, by now, direct ones. 'His daily bread', of course, reminds us of the Lord's Prayer, and, while highlighting the human concerns of that section of the prayer, hints to us also, as does the prayer, about the spiritual bread which was to be his and our mainstay. The main references to Christ's divinity are, however, more subtle. They are helped by the old convention (less used nowadays) whereby references to Christ are preceded by capital letters (He, His, etc.). In the first two stanzas these references have taken the usual form (His own decrees, His daily life), with Mary being referred to as 'His Mother'. In the last stanza, however, when the ordinariness of Jesus's childhood is being stressed, he is nevertheless referred to, triumphantly, in the very last word, as 'the Child'; and in the second line, when his birth is being referred to, he is described as 'the Undefiled' – a phrase which in itself contradicts the idea of ordinary human life, and stresses Christ's divine status.

The whole poem involves therefore a stressing of the reality of the Incarnation, while underlining that here an infinitely powerful God is submitting himself to the laws of the nature that he has created.

Reflections

How can God and man be contained within one person? We have already seen, in our meditations on the Crucifixion, just how important it was, in the divine scheme of things, that Jesus's Incarnation should be real, that he should suffer as a human being, and even share human beings' doubts and despair. Alice Meynell's short poem takes us to the heart of this mystery, at the moment of the Incarnation.

As one Person of the Trinity, Christ, the Word, has existed from the beginning of time. He was there, with the Father, at the Creation of the world. Yet, at one moment in historical time, he came to earth, to share in the experience of the mankind he had created; and in order to do so he had to obey the laws of nature, and be born a helpless child. Indeed, before that he had to be a foetus, developing within Mary's womb. And, even in that unformed, early stage, he was God almighty. The contrast is stupendous.

It reminds us of the importance of the material, real world. Have our visions of the divine order perhaps sometimes been too geared to the eternal, to the afterlife? The idea that this world is merely an antechamber, from which we eventually enter the eternal life, is an attractive one, particularly for those whose life in this world is burdensome. And we should never forget that Jesus came to give us 'the hope of eternal life'. But, by choosing to share our life in this world, is God telling us something of the importance of our earthly life as well? Would he have created us and the world merely to provide a testing ground which had no value except that of preparation for another world? By taking on flesh, has God validated the human condition? By becoming the Son of Man, has he helped us truly to become children of God?

The God we experience is not somewhere apart from us, viewing us with detachment amid all our troubles and tribulations in this world. He is there alongside us, sharing in our experiences, helping us with the example of his own sufferings. The old heretical distinction, made by the Manichaean sect, between a world of darkness governed by the forces of evil, and another world, beyond, which is governed by God and the forces of light, founders on the reality of the Incarnation. This is God's world, he is here in it with us, and he governs it as surely as he governs heaven. Jesus's Incarnation is not just a supernatural happening that took place in the past. It is an ever-present reminder that God is with us in our ordinary lives.

Christmas

God's gift to man

> Behold the father is his daughter's son:
> The bird that built the nest is hatched therein:
> The old of years an hour hath not outrun:
> Eternal life to live doth now begin,
> The word is dumb: the mirth of heaven doth weep:
> Might feeble is: and force doth faintly creep.

81

O dying souls, behold your living spring:
O dazzled eyes, behold your sun of grace:
Dull ears, attend what word this word doth bring;
Up, heavy hearts: with joy your joy embrace.
From death, from dark, from deafness, from despairs:
This life, this light, this word, this joy repairs.

Gift better than himself, God doth not know:
Gift better than his God, no man can see:
This gift doth here the giver given bestow:
Gift to this gift let each receiver be.
God is my gift, himself he freely gave me:
God's gift am I, and none but God shall have me.

Man altered was by sin from man to beast:
Beasts' food is hay, hay is all mortal flesh:
Now God is flesh, and lies in Manger pressed
As hay, the brutest sinner to refresh.
O happy field wherein this fodder grew,
Whose taste doth us from beasts to men renew.

(Robert Southwell, 'The Nativity of Christ', No. 6 in his *Sequence on the
Virgin Mary and Christ*)

Robert Southwell (*c.* 1561–95), born in Norfolk, was a Jesuit priest, educated at Douai and ordained in 1584, who landed in England in 1586. In 1589 he became domestic chaplain to the Countess of Arundel, but was arrested in June 1592 on the way to celebrate Mass. He was tortured continually during his imprisonment, which lasted almost three years, and was then executed at Tyburn on 21 February 1595. He was beatified in 1929 and canonized in 1970. His poems were mainly written during his short six-year mission in England. He clearly saw them as instruments in that mission. Their main theme is spiritual love, expressed in an often complicated style typical of the love poetry of the period, using striking figures of speech.

In style this poem is almost a complete antithesis to the one by Alice Meynell which we have just seen. Where Meynell's style is simple, Southwell's is complicated and intricate. Where Meynell is prepared merely to suggest further aspects of her thought, Southwell wishes to spell out every detail. There is no denying, however, that this is a very powerful poem which, by skilled use of the rhetorical figures of speech, and of wordplay, opens up for us new vistas of meaning. Some of the more mechanical-seeming conventions of the poetry of the sixteenth century here serve to underline that meaning.

The opening theme is similar to Meynell's: the paradox of the Creator becoming part of his own Creation. Southwell uses homely images to underline this. The father-creator has become the son of the daughter he had created; God is like a bird who has been hatched in the nest he had created. We then move on to the full import of the paradox: God is, in Old Testament terms, 'the Ancient of days', or 'the old of years', existing for ever; but he has now, as a baby, been living for only an hour. He, of life eternal, has only just begun to live. Christ is the Word, but he cannot speak. (Though 'Word' is not capitalized in the original text, the meaning is clearly Christ as the Word, the Second Person of the Trinity.) God is almighty, but he is a feeble child; he is all-powerful and strong, but as a child can only creep.

The second stanza moves from this mystery, to its effects on humanity. Southwell exhorts humankind to embrace the cures that Christ has provided for their ills. He here uses a typical sixteeenth-century poetic technique, called *versus rapportati* or *vers rapportés* (best translated as 'brought-back lines'), in order to list these effects. This technique had been particularly popular in France in the mid-sixteenth century, with poets like Jodelle and Ronsard, whose poetry he may of course have read during his exile. Each of the first four lines lists one aspect of fallen humanity, and the attribute of the incarnate Christ that heals it. Thus our '*dying* souls' behold a '*living* spring'; our *blinded* eyes behold a *sun* of grace; our *deaf* ears can hear the word brought by the Word (a pun being added for good measure); and our *heavy* hearts are full of *joy*. The four themes are thus death (cured by life), blindness (cured by light), deafness (cured by the Word) and despair (cured by joy). The two final lines of the stanza 'bring back' these four themes, listing, first of all, the ailments all together, and then the cures, in a typical *versus rapportati* pair of lists:

> From death, from dark, from deafness, from despairs,
> This life, this light, this word, this joy repairs.

Such techniques may seem ponderous and unreal to our modern eyes. But they were clearly very popular with

Renaissance audiences; and in this particular case, the technique is highly effective in expressing the all-embracing nature of Christ's 'repairing' of our ills.

The third stanza is the crux of the poem. We have considered the paradox of God made man, and we have measured all the benefits this has bestowed on humankind. Now we pause to wonder at the gift God has thereby given us, and to ponder on what our own reaction to this should be. Southwell here uses the noun 'gift' and the verb 'give' insistently, in a way that modern views of poetry would regard as poor practice. It is however a technique widely used in the sixteenth and seventeenth centuries, and is often, as here, both spectacular and highly effective. The repetitions bring out admirably the complications of the relationships involved. Each pair of lines produces an idea in relation to God, and its corollary in relation to humankind. Thus, in the first two lines, we have the initial simple idea that God could not have known a greater gift to give, than himself, and that man could not know a greater gift than his God. The next two lines complicate this with elaborate wordplay, based on the Latin formulae for the giving and receiving of gifts (e.g., 'donum dedit', or just 'd.d.', often written, together with the name of the giver and the recipient, on the flyleaf of books that have been given as a present). Here, the gift consists of the giver, 'given'. Humankind's response to receiving this gift should be to give themselves as a gift. The stanza ends with a declaration that, just as God freely gave himself as a gift, so we are God's gift, and must give ourselves wholly to him.

The last stanza returns to the theme of salvation, using the homely image of the hay in the manger. It raises the question of the nature of unregenerate man, no better than the animals, and of the humanizing influence of God's taking on of human nature. Men have been turned to beasts by sin; the hay in the manger is the symbol of this; Christ's lying in the hay is the sign of his taking on of humanity; this, the Incarnation, is what turns us back into men, from beasts.

Despite, indeed because of, all its complications, this poem is a powerful evocation of God's redeeming of the world through his Incarnation and Passion. It urges us to wake up to what has been offered to us, and it marvels at the priceless gift we have been given.

Reflections

One is reminded of the words (which we have seen earlier) written two centuries later, by Isaac Watts: 'Love so amazing, so divine, demands my soul, my life, my all.' The gift we have been given demands a response from us in the form of the gift of ourselves.

Following on from the last stanza, it is worth trying to imagine what, without the divine spark that we have been given, life in this world would be. We would truly be 'beasts' – driven by our desires, our selfish instincts, with no concern for others. The world would be a jungle. Yet within each of us God has put an instinct to good, a capacity to surmount our baser instincts. We may call this 'conscience'; but we Christians believe it to be the gift of the Holy Spirit, speaking to us from within. And it is what makes us truly human.

It would be tempting to ascribe all this to our Christian belief; and, indeed, Christian belief makes us particularly aware of what is going on within us, and enables us to rationalize and explain it, and consciously to have recourse to it. But it is part of God's infinite mercy that he has placed this instinct within all of us, believers and non-believers alike. It is part of the human condition of regenerated humankind.

It is possible, of course, to think of human beings who seem to have completely missed out on this instinct. Creators of genocide, for example. Is it possible to say of them that they are 'beasts', without any redeeming characteristics? While believing them to be aberrations from the human condition, it is also possible to think that, though the bases for their beliefs are distorted and dehumanized, they may nevertheless feel able to justify themselves to themselves. It is too easy to dismiss such people as monsters outside any normal human scale of values. What is particularly frightening about them is that they are *part* of humanity, that they *have* values, but that those values have been distorted beyond anything that would be normally acceptable to ordinary humans. In other words, they retain part of what we have been given, that separates us from being 'beasts'; but within this they have nevertheless become 'bestial'. It is for this reason that a study of such people, and their motivations, is essential if we are to learn how to combat such forces in the future. I believe, for example, that most people, when they wake up in the morning, look in the mirror and say to themselves 'I am all right; my attitudes and actions are justified.' And then some of these people go out and do, or get involved in, the most dreadful things. Only by trying to work out such people's reasons for action, or the justifications they make to themselves, can we learn how to deal with such people and attitudes.

Such problems are not easily resolved. It is perhaps worth thinking about specific examples of inhuman behaviour, and trying to assess whether there is such a thing as 'pure evil', in which man descends to the level of the beasts, or whether, in each case, there are some glimpses of the distorted *human* values which have led to inhuman results. We must also consider the fact that Jesus Christ has not only told us not to judge others, but that his teachings continually stressed the fact that his mercy and forgiveness are always available to anyone who repents. If Hitler had shown repentance in 1945, would we feel that God's forgiveness was justified? If we believe, with Southwell, that 'God is flesh . . . *the brutest sinner* to refresh', then we must accept that salvation was open to Hitler as much as to anyone else. No sin is ever too great for repentance to be refused.

To return to the main theme, however. God has turned us from beasts into humans. Belief in him can save us from many of the aberrations into which certain humans have stumbled, despite the offered gift of salvation. It is God made man who, by the reality of his human condition, has shared our condition and sanctified it. Through God we are are saved from death and despair. This is an unbelievable gift, given to us by an all-powerful God who has humbled himself for this purpose.

Christmas

A carol of joy and foreboding

'When He is King we will give Him the King's gifts,
    Myrrh for its sweetness, and gold for a crown,
Beautiful robes,' said the young girl to Joseph,
    Fair with her first-born on Bethlehem Down.

Bethlehem Down is full of the starlight –
  Winds for the spices, and stars for the gold,
Mary for sleep. And for lullaby music,
  Songs of a shepherd by Bethlehem fold.

When He is King they will clothe Him in grave-sheets,
  Myrrh for embalming, and wood for a crown,
He that lies now in the white arms of Mary,
  Sleeping so lightly on Bethlehem Down.

Here He has peace and a short while for dreaming,
  Close-huddled oxen to keep Him from cold,
Mary for love, and for lullaby music,
  Songs of a shepherd by Bethlehem fold.

(Bruce Blunt, 'Bethlehem Down')

Bruce Blunt (1899–1957) was a journalist and poet who was a close friend, and drinking companion, of the composer Peter Warlock (Philip Heseltine, 1894–1930). They often drank, with the artist Augustus John, in the Antelope, Chelsea, in the late Twenties (and were occasionally ejected for their drunkenness). That these two reprobates should have collaborated on a number of tender, moving religious songs (of which this is one of the best examples) appears paradoxical; but God moves in a mysterious way.

Christmas carols tend to be happy, straightforward songs of joy, and they have a place in the hearts of all Christians. Only rarely, however, can it be said that they move one deeply, despite the beauty of so many of them. In this section, I take a carol which has that special capacity to produce the shiver of unexplained pleasure in artistic expression. 'Bethlehem Down' (which appeared in the *Daily Telegraph* on Christmas Eve 1927) is of course difficult to imagine without the superb musical setting by Peter Warlock, with its apparently simple melody, enhanced by unusual and haunting harmonies. The poem itself, however, can stand on its own as a magical evocation of the mood of Christmas.

Blunt apparently claimed that this poem was 'rattled off' for Warlock, as a potboiler to meet the 'Christmas market', and that Warlock's own approach to it had been equally offhand. Warlock, in that period, had indeed decided to touch the popular market in order to earn some much needed cash, and carols had become one of his stocks-in-trade. Whatever the circumstances of the carol's creation, however, it is a very good example, both in its words and in its music, of almost instinctive inspiration.

What is evoked is a scene of pastoral calm. Like the primitive artists who depicted scenes from the life of Jesus, Blunt has transposed the events into a typical scene in his own country, with the Downs as its backdrop. The tone is, on the surface, that of folksong, with its simplicity and its repetitions. But, just as Warlock's music produces an apparently simple melody which is subtly complicated by the harmonies used, Blunt's text hides within the simple repetitions a series of minor variations which point to a profound and disturbing message.

The carol starts with an evocation of Christ's mother, simply described as 'the young girl'. Speaking to Joseph, she lists the royal gifts they will give Jesus 'when He is King'. Two of these gifts are those of the Magi – sweet-smelling myrrh, and gold from which to make his crown, together with a king's fine robes. The stanza is rounded off with the line, of which a variant is to be repeated later, 'Fair with her first-born on Bethlehem Down'.

This idyllic picture is continued in the second stanza, with the magic of the starlight, and the wind, providing the spices and gold of which she has spoken. And the sleeping Jesus is depicted, clinging to Mary, and lulled to sleep by the lullaby of a shepherd's song. Again, the final line provides a refrain which will be repeated later.

One has been lulled into expecting the mood, and the repetitions, to continue in the same vein. But the third stanza gives us a rude shock. 'When He is King', it starts, as though a continuation of the young mother's dream. And the first two lines mirror exactly the form of the same lines in the first stanza. But instead of fine clothes he will be clothed in grave-sheets; the myrrh will be there not as a sweet-smelling perfume, but as the spice for embalming a dead body; and instead of a crown of gold, he will have a wooden crown of thorns. Though we return to the present, and the sweet vision of the child sleeping in his mother's arms 'on Bethlehem Down', we have been starkly made aware of the nature of the kingship that awaits him, and of the suffering that he will have to undergo as he suffers and dies for humankind.

The final stanza contrasts the present with the future, and sees this as a precious time of peace before his ordeals. He has the oxen to keep him warm, his mother to provide love and – echoing the refrain of stanza 2 – the lullaby music of the shepherd's song.

This reminder of the true meaning of Christmas – that Christ came to earth to suffer – is starkly different from the general run of Christmas carols. It is as far from the saccharine vision of 'the little Lord Jesus' laying down 'his sweet head', 'away in a manger', as it is from the trendiness of 'Mary, blessed teenage mother'. The tone is gentle; in place of the exultant 'herald angels' singing, we have the quiet song of a shepherd. The scene is an intimate one, with a young mother dreaming about the future of her child. It is only momentarily that that tone, and that scene, are interrupted by the true vision of the future.

Reflections

The beauty of the scene at Bethlehem, as depicted to us by so many carols – is this sometimes in danger of deflecting us from the true message of the Incarnation? Jesus came to earth to share our experiences; he was born in a stable, to show how he embraced the lot of the poorest of the poor. That stable must have been filthy. The couple, who had travelled so far, must have been worn out, the pregnant Mary in particular, who could not even find anywhere until this to rest her head. And they were surrounded by animals, real animals amid all their muck. Even a carol like this, which cuts across the pure message of joy of Christmas, still presents us with an idyllic scene, with the stars and the lullaby music, and the 'close-huddled oxen to keep him from cold'. Was a stable chosen for Christ's birth because it was picturesque? What did it smell like? Were the shepherds the idealized rustics of traditional pastoral poetry, or real men of flesh and blood, of muck and sweat, with their own practical problems?

Yet it is perhaps the idealized picture of Bethlehem Down that brings out the underlying message of the poem more starkly. For Jesus's Incarnation came about in order that he might save us by his eventual suffering. The starkness of that message, the glimpse it gives us of the reality of Christ's experience, underlines the unreality of the conventional Christmas picture, and takes us with a jolt out of it. As

Lionel Johnson puts it, in a carol of his which achieves some of the same effects as Bethlehem Down, Jesus is the 'Lamb, who to sacrifice must pass', and 'Soon shall come Cross and Crown / In Salem Town' (Lionel Johnson, 'A Carol').[13]

Much of the sentimental picture of the Christmas in Bethlehem, then, can be an actual hindrance to our envisaging the reality of the Incarnation. If we try mentally to strip away all these unnecessary details, and just to consider the enormity of God almighty coming to earth to live as an ordinary human being, in an ordinary human environment, we can perhaps get nearer to the true meaning of Christmas.

13. For Lionel Johnson, see p. 62.

SECTION THREE

Aspects of Christian Experience

CHAPTER FIVE

Nature

A major theme in religious poetry is the perception of God which is vouchsafed to us by the world around us. To many, the marvels of nature are in themselves proofs of God. To others, perception of God requires insight of a particular kind, with humankind often unable, or able only with difficulty, to unravel the mysteries around them. I would like to start, however, with John Clare's simple, straightforward vision of the gratitude we should show to God for his creation, in his poem 'Summer Happiness':

> The sun looks down in such a mellow light
> I cannot help but ponder in delight
> To see the meadows so divinely lye
> Beneath the quiet of the evening sky
> The flags and rush in lights and shades of green
> Look far more rich than I have ever seen
> And bunches of white clover bloom again
> And plats of lambtoe still in flower remain
> In the brown grass that summer scythes have shorn
> In every meadow level as a lawn
> While peace and quiet in that silent mood
> Cheers my lone heart and doth my spirits good
> The level grass the sun the mottled sky
> Seems waiting round to welcome passers bye

Summer is prodigal of joy, the grass
Swarms with delighted insects as I pass
And crowds of grasshoppers at every stride
Jump out all ways with happiness their guide
And from my brushing feet moths flirt away
In safer places to pursue their play
In crowds they start. I marvel, well I may,
To see such worlds of insects in the way
And more to see each thing however small
Sharing joy's bounty that belongs to all
And here I gather by the world forgot
Harvests of comfort from their happy mood
Feeling God's blessing dwells in every spot
And nothing lives but ows him gratitude

John Clare (1793–1864), born in Helpstone, Northamptonshire, was the son of a farm labourer, and himself worked on the land. Though his parents were almost illiterate, he was a keen reader from early childhood, and started writing verse in his early teens. His first volume, *Poems Descriptive of Rural Life and Scenery* (1820), was highly successful and followed by three further volumes in the next 15 years. He had begun, however, to have fits of depression, and was admitted to an asylum in Epping in 1837. In 1841 he was admitted to Northampton General Lunatic Asylum, where he died in 1864. Though his poetry was neglected after his death, it has been much admired from the twentieth century onwards. His evocation of nature and landscape is highly personal, and couched in simple language that owes little to the artificial poetic diction of the 'nature poets' of the period.

Clare's simple language and idiosyncratic punctuation give us the impression of an uncomplicated countryman viewing nature directly, with no need for poetic language or complicated ideas. His vision is immediate, his eye open to every detail of the world around him.

The first stanza describes in detail the meadows in the summer sunshine, and declares how they 'cheer his lone heart' and 'do his spirits good'. By the second stanza, this happiness of the poet's is seen as being shared by nature itself. Though Clare appears so original and unaffected by the fashions of the poetry of his day, he does in fact use some of the contemporary poetic techniques, and here we find him indulging in the 'pathetic fallacy' criticized by Ruskin (the tendency among poets and artists of the late eighteenth and nineteenth centuries to ascribe human emotions to nature). So it is that he describes the grasshoppers and moths as 'sharing joy's bounty that belongs to all'; and their joy, in turn, produces further joy in the poet.

None of this, however, detracts from the poet's own sense of joy in nature, that breathes out of every phrase in this poem. It has been produced, Clare tells us, by God's blessing.

While many poets have expressed the same joy in nature, and, if Christians, have thanked God for this gift, there is an important step beyond this, which is not just to enjoy God's gifts, but to marvel at the way in which God has created everything so perfectly. Nobody has, I think, better expressed the wonderment of a human being at the marvels of creation than the Jesuit poet Gerard Manley Hopkins. One of the greatest examples of this is his poem 'Pied Beauty', in which he glories in the unusual textures of nature, and contrasts nature's ever-changing faces with the Creator, the God who never changes. Like Clare, he observes nature in great detail. He picks out one aspect only of Creation, 'dappled things' of varied colours and textures, and evokes some startling examples.

The poem speaks for itself, particularly with the dramatic last line, 'Praise him', which slows down the breakneck rhythm of the poem in a powerful, measured statement. The poem is full of Hopkins's typical effects – counter-rhythms, alliterations, assonances, wordplays, portmanteau (hyphenated) words, unusual words:

Glory be to God for dappled things –
    For skies of couple-colour as a brinded cow;
        For rose-moles all in stipple upon trout that swim;
Fresh-firecoal chestnut-falls; finches' wings;
    Landscape plotted and pieced – fold, fallow, and
    plough;
        And áll trádes, their gear and tackle and trim
All things counter, original, spare, strange;
    Whatever is fickle, freckled (who knows how?)
        With swift, slow; sweet, sour; adazzle, dim;
He fathers-forth whose beauty is past change:
                        Praise him.

Gerard Manley Hopkins (1844–89) was converted to Roman Catholicism while an undergraduate at Oxford in 1866. In 1868 he decided to become a Jesuit. Though at this stage he burned his poetry, believing it to be incompatible with the religious life, he later continued to write poetry, most of which was not published till after his death (by his friend the poet Robert Bridges). His poetry is highly original in its unusual rhythms ('sprung rhythm', scanned by accent or stress rather than by number of syllables), its skilful use of alliteration (repeated consonants) and assonance (repeated vowels), its often idiosyncratic choice of vocabulary, but above all the intensity of its thought and feeling.

God 'fathers-forth' the world in all its complexity. He, who is eternal and unchangeable, creates what is perpetually in flux and change. And yet, in every detail, God's Creation is a marvel of perfection. It contains an amazing system of checks and balances, which such thinkers as Keith Ward (in, for example, his book *God, Faith and the New Millennium*) have seen as the proof, through and not despite science, of the existence of God.

In another poem entitled 'To a Snowflake', Francis Thompson, a near-contemporary of Hopkins, similarly marvels at the ingenuity of the Creator, in even the smallest part of his Creation:

What heart could have thought you? –
Past our devisal
(O filigree petal!)
Fashioned so purely,
Fragilely, surely,
From what Paradisal
Imagineless metal,
Too costly for cost?
Who hammered you, wrought you,
From argentine vapour? –
'God was my shaper.
Passing surmisal,
He hammered, He wrought me,
From curled silver vapour,
To lust of his mind: –
Thou couldst not have thought me!
So purely, so palely,
Tinily, surely,
Mightily, frailly,
Insculped and embossed,
With His hammer of wind,
And His graver of frost.'

(Francis Thompson, 'To a Snowflake')

Francis Thompson (1859–1907) was a Roman Catholic from Lancashire, intended for the priesthood; but he was rejected because of his nervous timidity. He studied to become a doctor, but failed to qualify. In 1885, after being declared medically unfit for the army, he left home and went to London, where he lived as a homeless opium addict. In February 1887 he sent some of his poems to Wilfrid Meynell, a Catholic editor. Wilfrid not only published him; he and his wife Alice[14] rescued him from his life of destitution, organizing his life for him and providing constant encouragement. Three volumes of verse were published in the years 1893–97, and were very well received. He never rid himself entirely, however, of his addiction. He died of tuberculosis in 1907. His poetry is uneven, but the best of it is full of powerful imagery, and witnesses to his intense religious experience. One of his best-known poems is 'The Hound of Heaven'.

The short lines of this poem symbolize the apparently simple, tiny nature of the snowflake. At the same time the complexity of the thought contained in it reflects the marvellous, complicated perfection of the artefact. The first half of the poem is addressed to the snowflake itself by a wondering observer; the second half is the snowflake's response.

The initial question is one of wonderment: who could have created such a fragile and complex thing? Who could have even thought it up? It is beyond human comprehension ('past our devisal'). The words used to describe the snowflake all stress its fragility and complexity ('filigree', 'fragilely'), but also its purity. And with what sureness it has been created! The

14 For Alice Meynell, see p. 66.

list of adverbs conveys simply and concisely these complex ideas, much as the apparently simple exterior of the snowflake conceals its inner complexity. And what can it have been made of? The parallel with a smith creating something out of metal is central to the message; and that metal must be something unworldly, something carried over from the paradise of Eden.

The snowflake's reply starts with a simple answer to the initial question: 'God was my shaper.' The image of the smith is then continued. God has hammered it into shape, in an unimaginable way ('passing surmisal'). We then return to the question of the imagination, in words that echo the first line. The poet is addressed directly, and told that such a creation was beyond anything he could have imagined. The adverbs, as in the first part of the poem, mount up to depict the contrasting aspects of the nature of the artefact. It is tiny, but has been created with a sure hand. It is a frail, but mighty, creation. And the instruments God has used have been those of the world he has created: the hammer and engraving-tool of wind and frost.

*　　*　　*

What have we humans done, however, to the nature that God has given us? In another powerful poem, Gerard Manley Hopkins speaks of this:

> The world is charged with the grandeur of God.
>   It will flame out, like shining from shook foil;
>   It gathers to a greatness, like the ooze of oil
> Crushed. Why do men then now not reck his rod?
> Generations have trod, have trod, have trod,
>   And all is seared with trade; bleared, smeared with toil;
>   And wears man's smudge and shares man's smell: the soil

Is bare now, nor can foot feel, being shod.

And for all this, nature is never spent;
There lives the dearest freshness deep down things;
And though the last lights off the black West went
Oh, morning, at the brown brink eastward, springs –
Because the Holy Ghost over the bent
World broods with warm breast and with ah! bright wings.

(Gerard Manley Hopkins, 'God's Grandeur')

The impact of this poem rests on a strong contrast between the presence of God in nature, and man's effect upon that nature. The sonnet form is skilfully used to create this contrast.

The sonnet is a very strict form, originating in the Renaissance. Right up to our own day, it continues to be a favourite vehicle for those poets who find its form satisfying, and its constraints a challenge to their virtuosity. It consists of fourteen lines, of which the first eight are formed into two quatrains (usually, but not always, in the rhyme form abba abba). These are followed by six further lines, the sestet, containing two or three further rhymes. There is often a pause in the thought, between the quatrains and the sestet. A change of theme may also take place between the quatrains; and another typical procedure is to end the whole sonnet with a satisfying last two lines which sum up much of what has gone before.

In this particular sonnet, the first quatrain triumphantly evokes God's greatness. The second quatrain produces the contrasting, gloomy picture of man's apparent destruction of that greatness in nature. The poem is, however, rounded off in the sestet with an evocation of the continuing presence of God in nature, despite humankind's activities; and the last two lines powerfully evoke the presence of the Holy Spirit over everything.

Hopkins starts with a startling concept – that of God's greatness 'charging' the world.[15] The word can have a variety of meanings, and produces that ambiguity that is typical in Hopkins's poetry. It could, of course, mean that the world is 'charged' to tell of God's grandeur; it could also mean that it was 'challenged with' it; but a third possible meaning is that the world is 'charged' electrically with God's greatness. In 1877, when this poem was written, this would have been a remarkably modern image.

God's greatness 'flames out', 'shining'. The similes, 'like shining from shook foil', 'like the ooze of oil', are typically Hopkinsian in their unexpected and unusual nature. 'Shaken foil' does of course shine brightly, but the image is not one that would immediately come to mind to describe such shining. 'Like the ooze of oil / crushed' is even more odd, at first sight. It is only when one sees that the words 'crushed oil' are juxtaposed with 'shining' that one realizes that it refers to oil for lamps; crushed olive oil. The reference appears to be to a passage from Leviticus (24.1–4), where the Lord, speaking to Moses, says:

> Command the children of Israel, that they bring unto thee *pure oil olive beaten for the light*, to cause the lamps to burn continually. [. . .] [Aaron] shall order the lamps upon the pure candlestick before the Lord continually.

It is likely that Hopkins was using a translation other than the Authorized Version, most such translations using words

---

15. For some of these glosses on this poem, I am indebted to Walford Davies's excellent edition of Hopkins's poetry and prose (London: Everyman, 1998).

closer to his, e.g.: 'Order the Israelites to bring you crushed-olive oil.'

'Foil' and 'oil' both therefore refer to God's greatness 'shining forth', the world having been 'charged' with the telling of God to man. But what is the effect on man? The last line of the quatrain asks why, given all this, humankind has taken no notice of God's 'rod' – another ambiguous word, which can mean either God's rod of authority, or Christ's 'rood', his Cross. No doubt both meanings are implied, but the question remains: given the marvels of God, as revealed through nature, why does humankind ignore God?

The second quatrain now powerfully shows material-istic man's effect on the natural world. Its first line, with the desolate repetitions of 'have trod', depicts the dreary repetitive nature of unredeemed humanity's day-to-day existence. In the next line, 'trade', the materialism of the nineteenth century, is blamed. The choice of word, 'seared', is particularly telling. To 'sear' can mean to cause to dry up, or wither away; it can also mean to burn or char; but it also has (as the *Oxford English Dictionary* tells us) a theological meaning, to 'render the conscience incapable of feeling' (based on the verse from 1 Timothy 4.1–2: 'In the latter times some shall depart from the faith [. . .] speaking lies in hypocrisy; having their conscience seared with a hot iron'). All these meanings seem to be implied here. And, typically, Hopkins then piles on the epithets, insistently rhyming them with 'seared', 'bleared, smeared with oil', to convey, by the dreary repetition of sounds created by this, a world of dismal drudgery. (Note, however, that he does not do the obvious, and produce the words 'drear' or 'dreary'; one is left merely to sense them beneath the other verbs.) The impression is continued in lines 3 and 4 of the quatrain, with further dreary words, used in an unusual context: man's 'smudge' and 'smell' have contaminated nature. The soil is bare, and shoes have prevented man from feeling it.

But then comes the cry of hope, in the sestet. Despite all this, nature survives. Though it seems like the dusk of nature, with the lights going out in the West, new life 'springs' (like waters of 'dear freshness') in a new dawn to the East. And the poem ends with a magnificent allusion to the Holy Spirit, which at the Creation of the world 'moved upon the face of the deep' (Genesis 1.2), and which now 'broods' over the world which man has 'bent'. The theme of the brightness of God's presence is accentuated by the powerful mid-sentence exclamation 'ah!'.

Despite the gloomy picture of man's distortion of God's world, this poem glorifies God, as he is revealed in that very nature. It is man's blindness which shuns that revelation; but the Holy Spirit is always there, hovering over the world and making that revelation available to us, once we put the material behind us and open ourselves out to the spiritual.

★   ★   ★

When observing the world around us, many people have felt the same sense of mystery, the same form of mystical experience, that is provided for others by the experience of the arts. The French novelist Marcel Proust expresses this in a famous passage from his great novel *A la recherche du temps perdu*, in which he describes his hero, the young Marcel, standing in front of flowering hawthorns, trying in vain to explain the feelings he has experienced:

And then I returned to the hawthorns, and stood before them as one stands before those masterpieces which, one imagines, one will be better able to 'take in' when one has looked away for a moment at something else; but in vain did I make a screen with my hands, the better to concentrate upon the flowers, the feeling they aroused in me remained obscure and vague, struggling and failing to free itself, to float across and become one of them. They themselves offered me no enlightenment, and I could not call upon any other flowers to satisfy this mysterious longing.[16]

Proust's hero experiences, in nature, the same mysterious longing that Swann, another of Proust's characters, feels when he hears a particular 'little phrase' of music:

At a certain moment, without being able to distinguish any clear outline, or to give a name to what was pleasing him, suddenly enraptured, he had tried to grasp the phrase or harmony – he did not know which – that had just been played, and that had opened and expanded his soul, as the fragrance of certain roses, wafted upon the moist air of evening, has the power of dilating one's nostrils [. . .] It had all at once suggested to him a world of inexpressible delights, of whose existence, before hearing it, he had never dreamed, into which he felt that nothing else could initiate him.[17]

These feelings, in face of the wonders of nature or of the arts, are part of the experience of mankind as a whole, whether

16. Marcel Proust, *Du côté de chez Swann*, in the first volume of *A la recherche du temps perdu* (tràns. Moncrieff and Kilmartin; London: Folio Society, 1982, Vol. 1), p. 151.
17. Ibid., pp. 227–8.

Christian or not. But where people like Proust's heroes find difficulty in explaining to themselves exactly why they feel such things, for many Christians there is an answer to the mystery. For them, these 'high moments' of experience are when we indistinctly perceive God within his Creation, when, in R.S. Thomas's words, we can reflect upon the answer to a question we have not asked, 'A repetition in time of the eternal I AM' ('A Thicket in Lleyn') .

This sense of God's presence is forcibly expressed by Francis Thompson in one of his most successful poems, 'The Kingdom of God'. Here he sees that God's kingdom is not a distant thing, difficult to approach, but surrounds us in our ordinary existences, if we are only prepared to look, and to perceive. And this world is not just the world of beautiful nature. God can be revealed, too, even in the modern world, rejected by Hopkins, that humankind has created, 'seared with trade . . . bleared, smeared with toil . . . [wearing] man's smudge'. God, and his kingdom, do not exist far away from us, but alongside us, if only we were aware of it:

O world invisible, we view thee,
O world intangible, we touch thee,
O world unknowable, we know thee,
Inapprehensible, we clutch thee!

Does the fish soar to find the ocean,
The eagle plunge to find the air –
That we ask of the stars in motion
If they have rumour of thee there?

Not where the wheeling systems darken,
And our benumbed conceiving soars! –
The drift of pinions, would we hearken,
Beats at our own clay-shuttered doors.

The angels keep their ancient places; –
Turn but a stone, and start a wing!
'Tis ye, 'tis your estrangèd faces,
That miss the many-splendoured thing.

But (when so sad thou canst not sadder)
Cry; – and upon thy so sore loss
Shall shine the traffic of Jacob's ladder
Pitched betwixt Heaven and Charing Cross.

Yea, in the night, my Soul, my daughter,
Cry – clinging Heaven by the hems;
And lo, Christ walking on the water
Not of Gennesareth, but Thames!

(Francis Thompson, 'The Kingdom of Heaven')

The destitute, drop-out vagrant Thompson, who had so often slept rough in the centre of London, is keenly aware that he is surrounded even there by mystery. God is in everything in the material world; for Thompson he is revealed by our cry of sadness and despair, which brings him closer to us. The poem starts with a series of paradoxes in stanza 1; the kingdom of God is invisible, intangible, unknowable, ununderstandable; yet through our perception of the material world around us, we are able to see, touch, know and understand. Stanza 2 asks why we look elsewhere for that reality, and stanzas 3 and 4 speak of our deafness and blindness to all this, because we are 'estranged' from mystery. Then the dramatic last two stanzas, with the repetition of the word 'Cry', show that it is when we are sad and in despair, and cry out to God, that we can begin to see the kingdom of God more clearly. The images Thompson uses are startling, and the product of his London experiences.

The ladder that Jacob saw, in a dream, stretching from earth to heaven, with 'the angels of God ascending and descending on it' (Genesis 28.12) here stands for the perpetual presence of God's mystery among us, and the foot of it can stand just as easily at Charing Cross. And, for the soul that prays and cries to God, Christ is always present. He walks on the water of the Thames for those who live near that river, as he had walked on the Sea of Gennesareth, or Galilee, for his earliest disciples.

★　　★　　★

The experience of God in nature can differ widely from person to person. In some, it is akin to that revelation of 'something beyond reality' that the arts also provide. For others, it is the realization of the marvellous Creator, revealed in all the complexities of his Creation. And for yet others, it is the sense of mystery and of consolation to be found there, inexplicable yet sure. What gifts God has given us! – Not just the wonders of the world, but also the capacity we have been given to perceive through our senses, and understand through the miracle of our minds. All this is summed up by Thomas Traherne (1637–74) in a magnificent poem which, like so many of his, makes use of a lengthy list.[18] In this case the list is vast, and encompasses not only the wonders of nature, but also our senses that enable us to perceive it, the marvels of the human mind (even listing such things as the 'mariner's compass'), and the gift of human artistic creation. If all this is given to us here on earth, what can be intended for our souls in the hereafter?

18. See p. 124 for a note on Traherne, and on his use of lists.

For all the mysteries, engines, instruments, wherewith
the world is filled, which we are able to frame and
use to thy glory.

For all the trades, variety of operations, cities, temples,
streets, bridges, mariner's compass, admirable picture,
sculpture, writing, printing, songs and music,
wherewith the world is beautified and adorned.

Much more for the regent life,
And power of perception,
Which rules within.
That secret depth of fathomless consideration
That receives the information
Of all our senses,
That makes our centre equal to the heavens,
And comprehendeth in itself the magnitude of the
world;
The involv'd mysteries
Of our common sense;
The inaccessible secret
Of perceptive fancy;
The repository and treasury
Of things that are past;
The presentation of things to come;
Thy name be glorified
For evermore.

O miracle
 Of divine goodness!
O fire! O flame of zeal, and love, and joy!
Ev'n for our earthly bodies, hast thou created all things.
All things visible
All things material
All things sensible
 Animals,
 Vegetables,
 Minerals,
Bodies celestial,
Bodies terrestrial,
The four elements,
Volatile spirits,
Trees, herbs, and flowers,
 The influences of heaven,
Clouds, vapours, wind,
 Dew, rain, hail, and snow,
Light and darkness, night and day,
 The seasons of the year.
Springs, rivers, fountains, oceans,
Gold, silver, and precious stones.
 Corn, wine, and oil,
The sun, moon, and stars,
 Cities, nations, kingdoms.
And the bodies of men, the greatest treasures of all,
 For each other.
What then, O Lord, hast thou intended for our
Souls, who givest to our bodies such glorious things!

(Thomas Traherne, 'A Serious and Patheticall Contemplation of the Mercies
of God')

CHAPTER SIX

Suffering

And one said
Speak to us of love
And the preacher opened
his mouth and the word God
fell out so they tried
again speak to us
of God then but the preacher
was silent reaching
his arms out but the little
children the ones with
big bellies and bow
legs that were like
a razor shell
were too weak to come.

(R.S. Thomas, 'H'm')[19]

19. In R.S. Thomas, *Collected Poems 1945–1990* (London: Phoenix Giant, 1995). By kind permission of Mr Gwydion Thomas.

Ronald Stuart Thomas (1913–2000) was an Anglican priest from 1936 onwards, in various parishes of the Church in Wales. Though a fervent supporter of the Welsh language, he wrote all his poetry in English, his first language. Much of it is concerned with the quest for God – an uncertain quest, often bedevilled, or possibly aided, by doubt. His reputation, in modern English literature, ranks him with such giants as Eliot and Pound.

'H'm' is one of Thomas's bleakest poems. In it he graphically presents us with one of the greatest dilemmas faced by Christians. How can a loving God, who is all-powerful, allow the world to suffer in the way that it does? This concern has become even more urgent to many people in the wake of so many recent natural disasters, such as the 2004 tsunami or the various famines in Africa. The poem also highlights the problems Christian teachers have in attempting to provide explanations for those who are actually suffering – the awful tendency to descend into glibness.

The starkness of the statement, in this poem, is accentuated by the lack of punctuation, the short lines, the simple phrases. The preacher attempts to explain things in words, but is then forced to remain silent. He reaches out his arms, but then – in a startling use of a visual image – the whole of human suffering is evoked by the sight of the small starving children suffering from the terrible disease of kwashiorkor, caused by severe malnutrition, the distinguishing sign of which is the swollen bellies which we have become so accustomed to seeing on our television screens. If there is one image that summons up to our minds starving Africa, this is it.

Thomas pictures an enquiring world asking of a Christian teacher the nature of love. 'And the preacher opened his mouth and the word God fell out.' It is as though this is a stock reaction on the part of the preacher. He doesn't need to think. The word God just falls out of his mouth; it is a kind of cliché to which he turns every time the word 'love' is mentioned. But this does not satisfy the enquirers, 'so they tried again.' 'Speak to us of God, then,' they ask. But the preacher finds it impossible to do so. He is reduced to silently holding out his arms, in a gesture of love and caring. But the facts of the world belie what he is trying to convey. His love cannot reach those who are suffering in the world. And he is incapable of explaining it, of reconciling the idea of God, and of love, with it.

It is not just the natural disasters, the 'acts of God' as they are so ironically called, which we Christians find hard to explain. There are also the terrible injustices, the inhumanity of man to man: the Holocaust, the massacres in Rwanda and in Bosnia, the violence and terrorism in places like Israel, Palestine, Iraq. How can God have created a world in which people behave so appallingly to each other? Why do the wicked flourish? Why does evil exist? We are sometimes tempted to share the attitudes of the writer of Ecclesiastes:

> So I returned, and considered all the oppressions that are done under the sun: and behold the tears of such as were oppressed, and they had no comforter; and on the side of their oppressors there was power; but they had no comforter.
>
> Wherefore I praised the dead which are already dead more than the living which are yet alive.
>
> Yea, better is he than both they, which hath not yet been, who hath not seen the evil work that is done under the sun.
>
> (Ecclesiastes 4.1–3)

Something of that despair is to be found in the poems of the Israeli writer Yehuda Amichai, whose poem 'And there are days' speaks of the inexplicable absence of God from the terrible events of this world.

And there are days when everyone says, I was there
I'm ready to testify, I stood a few feet away from the
   accident,
from the bomb, from the crucifixion, I almost got hit,
   almost got crucified.
I saw the faces of bride and groom under the *chuppah*
   and almost rejoiced.
When David lay with Bathsheba I was the voyeur,
I happened to be there on the roof fixing the pipes,
   taking down a flag.
With my own eyes I saw the Chanukah miracle in the
   Temple,
I saw General Allenby entering Jaffa Gate,
I saw God.
And then there are days when everything's an alibi:
   wasn't there didn't hear
I heard the explosion only from a distance and I ran
   away, saw the smoke but
was reading a newspaper. I was staying in some other place.
I didn't see God, I've got witnesses.
And the God of Jerusalem is the eternal alibi God,
wasn't there didn't see didn't hear
was in some other place. Was some Place, some Other.

(Yehuda Amichai, 'And there are days', translated from the Hebrew by
Chana Bloch and Chana Kronfeld)[20]

20. First published in *Modern Poetry in Translation*, New Series, No. 14 (*Palestinian and Israeli Poets*), Winter 1998–99. By kind permission of *Modern Poetry in Translation*.

Yehuda Amichai (1924–2000) was born in Würzburg, Germany. His family emigrated to Palestine in 1935. He became Israel's leading poet. His poems have been translated into over 30 languages, and he is a literary figure of international stature.

The poem starts innocuously enough. It describes the very human desire to claim that one has been 'in on' great events. We have all done it in our time. Here, it starts with realistic events from everyday life: an accident, a wedding under the 'chuppah' or wedding canopy; but already the reality of life in the Israeli-Palestinian conflict comes to the fore with 'the bomb'. And suddenly one is caught up short, with the word 'crucifixion'. This takes us from the present to the past, from present suffering to past suffering; and in its use of a Christian symbol shows us the universality of such experience.

Note the phrases used to insist to the hearer that one is speaking the truth: 'I'm ready to testify'; 'With my own eyes'. Note, too, the extensive use of the word 'almost': 'I almost got hit, almost got crucified'; 'I saw the faces [. . .] and almost rejoiced.' These people are claiming acquaintance with events, but only as observers, partly detached from the reality of what they are observing.

The mention of a crucifixion leads us from the scenes of modern life, and we now visit some of the most famous episodes in Jewish history – or at least some of the most well known in popular memory: David's seduction of Bathsheba on the rooftop; the miracle of 'Chanukah', the tiny jug of oil that kept the eternal light, 'N'er Tamid', lit for eight days at the time of Judas Maccabeus's rededication of the Temple (commemorated now by the eight-day 'Festival of

Lights'); and, from more recent history, the British General Allenby's triumphant entry into Jerusalem in 1917,[21] ending Turkish rule. One is reminded of 'Dai's boast', in David Jones's First World War poem *In Parenthesis*, where the Welsh infantryman claims to have been at all past battles of the Welsh people. These similar claims to have 'been there' are extravagant, and absurd. They are, however, rounded off by a stark, simple statement. 'I saw God.'

For a member of the Jewish religion, this is a shocking statement. In the Bible, actually to see God was forbidden to ordinary humans, to the extent that Elijah, going out of his cave at the call of the 'still, small voice' which denoted the presence of God, had to 'wrap his face in his mantle' (1 Kings 19.13). Even to Christians, the claim to have 'seen God', when we have been told that in this world we are only able to 'see through a glass darkly', and that it is only at the end of time that we shall 'see face to face', is almost blasphemous. The poet has put it here as the climax of the fantasies of those he is describing, and a proof of their unreality; but also in order to lead us into the eventual evocation of the elusiveness of God.

We now come to the theme of the 'alibi'. This is not a mere acceptance that one was not there, but a positive desire to prove it. The word 'alibi' suggests a guilt that one is trying to avoid. Again phrases are produced to bolster up this new account: 'I've got witnesses.' The alibi is needed in relation to an act of terrorism, 'the explosion'. But it is also needed in relation to the idea that one might have seen God in all this.

And then comes the pivotal moment in the poem. We turn from the ordinary people of this world, with their need for alibis, to God. But God, too, is an 'alibi God'. He was

21. Louis Massignon, one of the people to whom this book is dedicated, shared a vehicle with Lawrence of Arabia in Allenby's procession into Jerusalem.

not present at the events in Jerusalem, the bombings and the terrorism. He too protests his innocence: 'wasn't there didn't see didn't hear was in some other place'. The childishness of the denials is underlined by the lack of punctuation; it is as though a child is breathlessly denying responsibility for something. Finally, that 'other place' is defined by capital letters: 'some Place, some Other'. God's in his heaven, all's wrong with the world.

This bleak vision is one form of human reaction to the problem of the world's suffering and of God's omnipotence. But – and it cannot be stressed enough – it requires a belief in God in order even to arrive at this apparent impasse. For the atheist, there is no problem at all. The world is just a terrible place, and that's it. The thinking believer, however, is perpetually assailed by the problem of God and his world.

Many of the Church's teachings on this matter, over the ages, have been unsatisfactory. The cult of suffering in the Catholic Church in late nineteenth-century France, for example, with its stress on the heroic 'assuming' of suffering for mystical purposes, and the sharing in Christ's mission by individuals taking on suffering to expiate the sins of the world, seems to the modern eye unhealthy. One of its typical results was the decision, by some extreme believers, to go to Lourdes to pray not for healing, but for sickness.

Elements of such beliefs continue to subsist in some areas of the universal Church. Modern theologians, however, tend to see suffering far more as a necessary, but unpleasant, part of the business of being a human being. Rabbi Jonathan Sacks, for example, in the immediate aftermath of the 2004 tsunami disaster, wrote a thoughtful article in which he described the explanation, given by a teacher of his, of our inability to penetrate God's inscrutable intentions. If we could see such things from the viewpoint of God, he said, 'we would understand divine purpose but at the cost of ceasing to be human':

> We would accept all, vindicate all, and become deaf to the cries of those in pain. God does not want us to cease to be human, for if He did, He would not have created us. We are not God. We will never see things from His perspective. The attempt to do so is an abdication of the human situation.
>
> (*The Times*, 8 January 2005)

Our job, Sacks went on, is not to understand, not to be reconciled to the pain and suffering of the world, but to 'strive for good in the short term, not just the long; in this world, not in the next; from the perspective of time and space, not infinity and eternity. God asks us not to understand but to heal; not to accept suffering but to diminish it.'

A disaster such as the one he was referring to is thus seen as an occasion not just for grief and sorrow, but also for action. In the reactions of so many people to this and similar disasters, one can find a vindication of humanity, with all the best in human nature coming to the fore. Archbishop Robert Runcie, in a sermon given after the Zeebrugge ferry disaster, quoted someone who had been in the midst of the disaster as saying:

> Tragedy does not take away love: it increases it. Perhaps we are more loving people, more sensitive, more concerned for each other because of that moment of grief which overthrew our ideas of what things matter, and opened our eyes again to the importance of our common humanity.
>
> ('Zeebrugge Ferry Disaster', *The Times Greatest Sermons of the Last 2000 Years*)

It is hard to imagine a world without suffering. If such a world existed, humankind would have no yardstick by which to measure its own humanity. A poem by Thomas Traherne takes us to the centre of this dilemma.

Were all the World a Paradise of Ease
   'Twere easie then to live in Peace.
Were all men Wise, Divine and Innocent,
   Just, Holy, Peaceful and Content,
      Kind, Loving, True and alwaies Good,
      As in the Golden Age they stood,
        'Twere easie then to live
In all Delight and Glory, full of Love,
   Blest as the Angels are above.

But we such Principles must now attain,
   (If we true Blessedness would gain)
As those are, which will help to make us reign
   Over Disorders, Injuries,
      Ingratitudes, Calamities,
      Affronts, Oppressions, Slanders, Wrongs,
        Lies, Angers, bitter Tongues,
The reach of Malice must surmount, and quell
   The very Rage, and Power of Hell.

(Thomas Traherne, from *Christian Ethicks*, 1675)

Thomas Traherne (1637–74) was the son of a Hereford shoemaker, but was brought up after his father's death by a wealthier relative. He attended Hereford Cathedral School and Brasenose College, Oxford. He was ordained as an Anglican priest in 1660, and became Rector of Credenhill, Herefordshire. From 1667 he was personal chaplain to Sir Orlando Bridgman, Lord Keeper of the Great Seal. Most of his poetry was discovered in the 1890s, and finally made him famous two centuries after his death. He was very devout, and his poetry, particularly that concerned with nature, expresses a firm faith, and a joy in creation.

Traherne starts by imagining a world without sin, in which all men are perfect. To underline his point he gives a long list of the qualities which would make up this perfection. In much of Traherne's poetry, lists are a powerful technique. In this case the list, indigestible as it seems, is important to the poem's meaning, in that it gives rise to the equally indigestible, but highly effective, contrasting list in the second stanza. If all the world were like a paradise, he says, like the paradise of Eden before sin came into the world, it would be easier to live good, loving lives, like the angels. (Note that, like many writers of the sixteenth and seventeenth centuries, he equates the 'Golden Age' described by the Ancients with the paradise on earth described in the Bible.)

This makes one think what such a world would be like. It is interesting to note how unconvincing the utopias are, that various writers have described over the centuries. This has led, in the twentieth century, to the production of a series of 'dystopian', or anti-utopian, novels and stories. In a number of them, such as Aldous Huxley's novel *Brave New World* (1932), and Julian Barnes's short story 'The Dream' (1989), the corrosive and destructive effect of a world devoted to unremitting happiness is described. Julian Barnes's hero, in a heaven where everything always goes right for him, realizes that to have his favourite football team always winning gets rid of any of the real pleasure afforded by them winning when they had occasionally lost, and that, having improved his golf to the extent of doing every round in 18 shots, there is nothing else to aim for. And he also realizes that something is missing:

> I wanted to be *judged*, do you see. It's what we all want, isn't it? I wanted, oh, some kind of summing-up. I wanted my life looked at. [. . .] I'm a normal person, and I just wanted what a lot of normal people want. I wanted my life looked at.

('The Dream', in *A History of the World in 10¹/₂ Chapters*, p. 293)

A world in which everything went right, in which there was no suffering, no sin, would have little meaning. It is part of the human condition to live in an imperfect world, which alone can give meaning to our lives.

Having produced this unreal dream in the first stanza, Traherne turns in the second stanza to the reality of the world, 'now', in the sense of the 'now' in St Paul's contrast between this world and the next: 'For now we see through a glass darkly; but then face to face.' (1 Corinthians 13.12). 'But we such Principles must *now* attain.' In this world, full of the great list of 'disorders, injuries, ingratitudes, calamities', etc., which he now produces, we must struggle, through principles which help us to overcome these things, in order to attain that state of blessedness which would be so easy without sin.

What should these principles be? In the two last stanzas from the next poem from the same volume, Traherne outlines them to us:

If we would to the Worlds distemper'd Mind
    Impute the Rage which there we find,
We might, even in the midst of all our Foes,
    Enjoy and feel a sweet Repose.
    Might pity all the Griefs we see,
    Anointing every Malady
      With precious Oyl and Balm;
And while ourselves are Calm, our Art improve
    To rescue them, and shew our Love.

O holy Jesus who didst for us die
    And on the Altar bleeding lie,
Bearing all Torment, pain, reproach and shame,
    That we by vertue of the same
    Though enemies to GOD, might be
    Redeem'd, and set at libertie.
      As thou didst us forgive,
So meekly let us Love to others shew,
    And live in Heaven on Earth below!

(Thomas Traherne, from *Christian Ethicks*)

Love is the answer, says Traherne. We can achieve that repose and calm, which would come so easily to those in paradise, by our efforts here on earth. We can, as he triumphantly says in the last line, 'live in Heaven on Earth

126

below' if we show love to others, if we show pity to those who grieve, if we pour 'oil and balm' over every ill. If we remain calm in the face of the forces of this world, we can do good to others, through our love. Jesus has shown us the way, by his 'torment, pain, reproach and shame' on our behalf. Through him we can, even if we are sinners ('enemies to God'), be redeemed both by his love and by our own.

Robert Runcie, in his Zeebrugge sermon, made much the same point when he said:

> It is in the selfless heroism of so many at Zeebrugge that we can see God's love at work. For the God and Father of our Lord Jesus Christ is not a God who stands outside us, and sends disaster. He is not even a God who offers comfort from a distance. He is Immanuel, God with us, the God who in Christ crucified plunges into the darkness of human sorrow and suffering, to stand alongside us, even in death. Christian faith does not mean believing in impossible things. It means trusting that Christ's promises never fail. 'Though a man die, yet shall he live.' Faith is not hoping that the worst won't happen. It is knowing that there is no tragedy which cannot be redeemed.
>
> (Runcie, 'Zeebrugge Ferry Disaster')

In other words, God is here with us, in our suffering. Jesus's coming into the world did not mean that the world would change overnight, but that *people* would change, if and when they accepted the message he had brought. Thus it is that suffering can bring us to good, can help us to have compassion for others, can bring to the fore the godlike within us.

While such arguments are often intellectually satisfying, they can prove inadequate when we are faced with the raw grief of the recently bereaved. The explanation that, for the Christian, one of the consolations for grief and suffering can be the knowledge that Christ, on the Cross, shared our sufferings, that God is not 'out there', impervious to our condition, but 'in here', sharing it, can seem irrelevant in the presence of immediate grief. Are these perhaps just theologians' arguments, no doubt true in themselves, but which do not speak to ordinary people? One of the characters in a novel by the French author François Mauriac is described thus: 'The misery, the wounded nature of man, which might have inclined Costadot's religious nature towards solutions of a mystical order, in fact did the opposite; he was too little a theologian to be satisfied with arguments which absolved the Creator from having created such an abject creation' (Mauriac, *Les Chemins de la mer*, 1939).

Though many sufferers are sustained by their faith, there are many others for whom even the firmest faith cannot withstand the pain of loss, the gripping torment of despair. In one of her most striking poems, Emily Dickinson describes her own grief, and wonders whether Christ's sufferings were anything like her own.

I measure every Grief I meet
With narrow, probing, Eyes –
I wonder if It weighs like Mine –
Or has an Easier size.

I wonder if They bore it long –
Or did it just begin –
I could not tell the Date of Mine –
It feels so old a pain –

I wonder if it hurts to live –
And if They have to try –
And whether – could They choose between –
It would not be – to die –

I note that Some – gone patient long –
At length, renew their smile –
An imitation of a Light
That has so little Oil –

I wonder if when Years have piled –
Some Thousands – on the Harm –
That hurt them early – such a lapse
Could give them any Balm –

Or would they go on aching still
Through Centuries of Nerve –
Enlightened to a larger Pain –
In Contrast with the Love –

The Grieved – are many – I am told –
There is the various Cause –
Death – is but one – and comes but once –
And only nails the eyes –

There's Grief of Want – and Grief of Cold –
A sort they call 'Despair' –
There's Banishment from native Eyes –
In sight of Native Air –

And though I may not guess the kind –
Correctly – yet to me
A piercing Comfort it affords
In passing Calvary –

To note the fashions – of the Cross –
And how they're mostly worn –
Still fascinated to presume
That Some – are like My Own –

(Emily Dickinson, 'I measure every Grief')

The American poet Emily Dickinson (1830–86), after a perfectly sociable early life, gradually withdrew from her late twenties onwards into her own inner world. She wrote almost 2,000 short poems, for which she unsuccessfully sought publication (only seven being published in her lifetime). They were discovered, and published, after her death. Originally considered an eccentric, bewildering poet, she is now accepted as a major writer, with unusual and original forms of expression. Much of her poetry reflects an inner distress, in a Christian context.

The deceptively simple verse-form, the short sentences, the disjointed forms of expression punctuated by dashes, all convey vividly the dull despair of the sufferer. One of the strengths of this poem is the way in which the poet succeeds in giving a convincing depiction of her own grief, without describing it directly. Instead, we find her looking at other people, wondering if their grief can be anything like hers. Her 'narrow, probing eyes' show the intensity of her search. Everyone, and everything, she sees is subjected to this scrutiny, in the self-absorption typical of a depressive, for whom every-thing in the world is subordinated to his or her own feelings.

She wonders if they suffer as much as she does (using the solid image of weight, so expressive of the mental weighing-down of such grief), and how long it has lasted. This leads her to the only description, in the poem, of her own grief.

Typically, it is in the form of a statement expressing her own lack of knowledge about it: 'I could not tell the Date of Mine – It feels so old a pain.'

In the third stanza, the pain of living, and the possibility of choosing to die, evoke the temptation of suicide. But, again, this is expressed in the form of a question as to whether other people have felt the same urge to die. It is as though the poet, needing to discuss these things, is nevertheless unable to describe them in terms of her own experience.

The next three stanzas deal with the possibility of a relief from this suffering. Some people seem to smile again. Can the years heal? Or – and here the unusual image is particularly striking – will they go on 'aching still through Centuries of Nerve'? The ache of grief is here compared to that created by a damaged nerve, in a vivid physical comparison like the earlier one of weight.

She then goes into the various forms of grief, with the phrase 'I am told' distancing the poet, who has to rely on the experience of others. Prominent among them is 'a sort they call "Despair"'. Note the distancing effect of this phrase, which presumably refers to the form of grief from which she herself suffers. It is as though every time, in this poem, that she comes near to her own case, she has to distance herself from it.

We now come to the climax of the poem. Dickinson evokes Christ's suffering on the Cross. This evocation is, however, couched still in words of uncertainty. 'Though I may not guess the kind – Correctly', 'still fascinated to presume'. Nevertheless, the Cross provides comfort – indeed, in another unusual phrase, this is 'a piercing Comfort', something vital and dramatic. The way in which Calvary is introduced is strangely like the way in which she has been observing those around her, to weigh their grief.

Here, she is 'passing Calvary', and almost as though she has come on it by chance, she 'notes' what she sees. And what she sees is described in prosaic human terms as well. She refers to the 'fashions' of the Cross, and how they are 'worn'; in other words, the outward appearances of suffering. And she is 'fascinated', and led to 'presume' (much as she had been presuming things about those around her), from those appearances, that some of those sufferings may be like her own.

Dickinson's poem conveys graphically the dull ache of grief, and the self-absorption of the griever, who sees the whole world through the eyes of his or her own suffering. It conveys, too, the Christian's attempt to see the Cross of Christ as a consolation, in that Christ came to this world to suffer like us. That attempt is, however, tentative and uncertain, in face of the gnawing immediacy of personal suffering.

This evocation by Dickinson of the example of Christ on the Cross is typical of many attempts, in poetry, to deal with the mystery of suffering, in that it is expressed not in clear certainties, but in tentative explorations of what may be true. This is, indeed, a reflection of our own situation in relation to suffering. When faced by someone in the depths of grief, it is tempting to speak in certainties, to produce the glib answers that trip only too readily from our tongues. But the grieving are not helped by such statements. It sometimes seems as though we are insulting their grief by trying too hard. And often we are also misleading ourselves. Perhaps what is needed is less certainty, and more mutual exploration of what may be.

In this chapter, we have looked at some of the problems surrounding the question of suffering – problems which often seem exacerbated, rather than helped, by our Christian faith. The poems that we have examined provide, perhaps, a starting-point for further exploration of what is a never-ending quest.

CHAPTER SEVEN

Doubt

No worst, there is none. Pitched past pitch of grief,
More pangs will, schooled as forepangs, wilder wring.
Comforter, where, where is your comforting?
Mary, mother of us, where is your relief?
　My cries heave, herds-long; huddle in a main, a chief-
woe, world-sorrow; on an age-old anvil wince and sing –

Then lull, then leave off. Fury had shrieked 'No ling-
ering! Let me be fell: force I must be brief'.
　O the mind, mind has mountains; cliffs of fall
Frightful, sheer, no-man-fathomed. Hold them cheap
May who ne'er hung there. Nor does long our small
　Durance deal with that steep or deep. Here! creep,
Wretch, under a comfort serves in a whirlwind: all
Life death does end and each day dies with sleep.

(Gerard Manley Hopkins, 'No worst, there is none')

The most devout of believers can succumb to doubt; and
that doubt can lead to deep despair. This poem by Hopkins
expresses that despair so heartrendingly that it is hard to

believe that this is the same poet who wrote the joyful hymns to God's glory, of which we have seen two in an earlier chapter.[22] In 1884–85, during his time as Professor of Greek and Latin Literature at University College Dublin, Hopkins went through a period of physical and spiritual collapse, brought on in part by the stresses of the post, but above all by a questioning of the very bases of his faith. This led to the writing of what have been called the 'terrible sonnets' of 1885, of which the above is an example.

Though this is written in the same sonnet form as his calmer poems of other days, that form here appears to be being torn asunder, in sympathy with his mood. The thoughts burst beyond the confines of the lines, as hyphenated words straddle the line-endings, and even an ordinary word such as 'lingering' is torn in half across the lines. The whole impression is of someone thrashing around in torment.

The first statement, 'No worst, there is none', sets the tone. Every time he thinks that this is the worst experience he has ever been through, things get even worse. He has been 'pitched past pitch of grief'. Typically, even now Hopkins is using words that can have a variety of meanings. One meaning is that he has been 'thrown' into depths of grief – a meaning that would go well with the images, later in the poem, of falling and cliffs. But it could also imply 'blackness', thrown into greater darkness than pitch; or it could imply sound, the cries we hear later in the poem being at a greater pitch (and the 'wilder (w)ringing' of his grief); or it could refer to the highly-strung nature of his own nervous system, attacked by the pangs of despair. All these meanings describe the overwhelming nature of his experience. He turns to the Holy Spirit, 'the Comforter',

22. For a short note on Gerard Manley Hopkins, for two of his earlier sonnets and for a discussion of the nature of the sonnet-form, see p. 100–1, 104–6.

and finds no help there. He turns to the Virgin Mary, our intercessor with God, and the result is the same.

Now, in the second quatrain, he describes his own reaction, the cries of grief which have been hammered out of him on the anvil of despair. The alliteration in 'h', 'heave, herds-long; huddle . . .' gives the impression of these panting cries, while the animal imagery of cattle huddling together shows how much his thoughts are like dumb animals driven together by outside forces. Those forces are now personified, as 'Fury', whose cries vie with his as she shrieks that she must be 'fell' ('cruel, ruthless, savage', *OED*) and swift. Here, the alliteration in 'f', 'fell: force . . . brief', conveys the hissing of the poisonous Fury.

Finally, in the sestet, Hopkins gives a graphic picture of the nature of despair. The repetition of the word 'mind' conveys the insistent, numbing nature of his thought. In his despair he is falling, falling, as in a nightmare. The mind is full of cliffs so steep and deep that no man could measure them. And they are so real to those who suffer that only those who have not suffered in this way can make light of them. The imagery, in these six lines, has been likened to that of *King Lear*, and certainly, after the evocation of the cliffs (which remind us of Gloucester on the clifftop), we have, without any precise textual reference it must be admitted, a mood which parallels that of Lear and the Fool on the blasted heath, creeping under shelter. That 'shelter' is, ominously, the only comforting thought, that life will end with death.

The nightmare sensation of endlessly falling, which is evoked in this poem, is one which many people have expressed when talking about their despair, as is the sense of being in great depths. In David Gascoyne's 'De Profundis', for example, we find much the same mood as Hopkins's:

Out of these depths:

Where footsteps wander in the marsh of death and an
Intense infernal glare is on our faces facing down:

Out of these depths, what shamefaced cry
Half choked in the dry throat, as though a stone
Were our confounded tongue, can ever rise:
Because the mind has been struck blind
And may no more conceive
Thy throne . . .

Because the depths
Are clear with only death's
Marsh-light, because the rock of grief
Is clearly too extreme for us to breach:
Deepen our depths

And aid our unbelief.

(David Gascoyne, 'De Profundis', from 'Miserere')[23]

---

23. In David Gascoyne, *Collected Poems 1988* (Oxford and New York: Oxford
University Press, 1988). By kind permission of Oxford University Press.

David Gascoyne (1916–2001) spent much of the pre-war period in Paris, where he associated with the Surrealist poets, whom he did much to bring before the British public, while himself writing Surrealist poetry. His third collection, *Poems 1937–42* (1943), contained a certain amount of religious poetry, described by Cyril Connolly as taking us 'as near the precipice as a human being is able to go and still turn back'. Between 1954 and 1964 he was affected by writer's block, and produced very little; then, after a breakdown, he spent most of the next 11 years in psychiatric hospitals, in one of which he was cared for by his future wife Judy, marriage to whom restored his self-esteem. Thereafter he returned to writing and publishing.

It is interesting that Connolly's comment on Gascoyne should have used the image of the precipice. Gascoyne's poem reflects the same nightmare scenario as Hopkins's. The poet is in infernal depths so deep that there is no way out but to go deeper. He addresses the God whom he now cannot conceive, because his mind has been blinded. His cries cannot even get out of his dry throat. Yet he manages to pray to God: 'Aid our unbelief.'

This capacity, on the part of the Christian cast into doubt, still to address himself or herself to the God in whom he or she cannot now believe, shows the extent to which such doubt and despair forms part of a Christian faith. The more profound the belief, it appears, the more the mind is open to doubt. Some of the greatest mystics – St Teresa of Avila, St John of the Cross – have had 'dark nights of the soul' in which all has seemed pointless. St Teresa is an extreme case. Though doubting the existence of God, she continued with her daily prayers, day after day, week after week, month after month, until her faith returned.

Gascoyne's poetry on this subject contains the same sense of longing for the return of faith. But for him (as we see in another poem, 'Ex Nihilo') that faith will have to be founded on 'the debris of all certainties'. In other words, doubt is what can clear away all unreal certainties, in order to provide a solid base, 'the hardest stone', on which to found faith.

Here am I cast down
Beneath the black glare of a netherworld's
Dead suns, dust in my mouth, among
Dun tiers no tears refresh: am cast
Down by a lofty hand,

Hand that I love! Lord Light,
How dark is Thy arm's will and ironlike
Thy ruler's finger that has sent me here!
Far from Thy face I nothing understand,
But kiss the Hand that has consigned

Me to these latter years where I must learn
The revelation of despair, and find
Among the debris of all certainties
The hardest stone on which to found
Altar and shelter for Eternity.

(David Gascoyne, 'Ex Nihilo', from 'Miserere')[24]

24. In David Gascoyne, *Collected Poems, 1988* (Oxford and New York: Oxford University Press, 1988). By kind permission of Oxford University Press.

Gascoyne feels that it is God himself who has 'cast him down' (an image which continues the idea of falling). And, like St Teresa, he still, amid unbelief, has an inkling of the nature of God, even when he is far from his face. It is God who has consigned him to this despair; but (in a significant phrase) that despair is a 'revelation'. It has destroyed the easy certainties of a shallow Christian belief, and amid the rubble caused by that destruction one can seek out a rock on which to found true faith, which is an altar to worship God, and a shelter from despair, for all eternity. Gascoyne has here moved beyond the despair of Hopkins, whose 'shelter' was merely the comforting thought of death.

In another sonnet Hopkins similarly reacts against his own despair, looking to God, struggling with him, in order to escape:

Not, I'll not, carrion comfort, Despair, not feast on thee;
Not untwist – slack they may be – these last strands of
    man
In me ór, most weary, cry *I can no more.* I can;
Can something, hope, wish day come, not choose not
    to be.
But ah, but O thou terrible, why wouldst thou rude on
    me
Thy wring-world right foot rock? lay a lionlimb against
    me? scan
With darksome devouring eyes my bruisèd bones? and
    fan,
O in turns of tempest, me heaped there; me frantic to
    avoid thee and flee?
Why? That my chaff might fly; my grain lie, sheer and
    clear.
Nay in all that toil, that coil, since (seems) I kissed the
    rod,
Hand rather, my heart lo! lapped strength, stole joy,
    would laugh, chéer.
Cheer whom though? The hero whose heaven-
    handling flung me, fóot tród
Me? or me that fought him? O which one? is it each
    one? That night, that year,
Of now done darkness I wretch lay wrestling with (my
    God!) my God.

(Hopkins, 'Not, I'll not, carrion comfort, Despair')

Here Hopkins rejects that despair which feasts off his dead
emotions and provides a kind of distorted comfort. As in
the previous poem, however, the strength of his emotions
is shown by repeated words, by exclamations within the

sentences, by daring enjambements which carry sentences over from line to line.

He will no longer cry 'I can no more' ('No worst, there is none'). The repetitions of the word 'can' show the effort to prove his capability to cast off despair. He *can* hope, *can* look to a new dawning, *can* reject the idea of suicide (evoked in a reference to Hamlet's speech on suicide, 'To be or not to be').

In the second quatrain he turns to God himself, who (in a parallel to Gascoyne's words) has 'cast him down'. The reference to God is typically exclamatory and repetitive: 'But ah, but O thou terrible . . .'. He asks why God has done this to him. The imagery is powerful, with him, the victim, who was frantic to avoid God's power, 'heaped there' (an image which reminds us of his earlier image of his cries being like cattle 'huddled' together), like grain waiting to be 'fanned'.

The real drama comes, though, in the sestet, which starts with the stark word 'Why?'. In an attempted explanation of why God has done this to him, the poet continues to use the image of the threshing floor, and purification through threshing. In St Matthew's Gospel we read that God's 'fan is in his hand, and he will thoroughly purge his floor, and gather his wheat into the garner; but he will burn up the chaff with unquenchable fire' (Matthew 3.12). Hopkins uses the same imagery to suggest that perhaps God has put him through all his suffering in order to get rid of all that is impure (the chaff), so that what is left will be his grain, 'sheer and clear'. When this theme was first introduced, at the end of line 7, the word 'fan', significantly, was picked out, separated from the rest of its sentence, at the end of the line. This idea of winnowing away the impurities, and leaving behind the pure self, echoes Gascoyne's idea of the clearing away of unreal certainties, in order to create a proper basis for faith.

The final image of the poem is highly dramatic. Like Jacob wrestling with the angel (or with God), the poet has, since he 'kissed the rod' (the rood, or Cross), been struggling with Christ, 'the hero'. The last line of the poem, with its sudden exclamation in brackets repeating the phrase 'my God!' shows a dawning realization, in Hopkins, that the dreadful struggles of 'that night, that year' in which all had been black for him, had in fact been struggles with God. The emergence, here, from the dead despair of his other 'terrible sonnets' is shown by the phrase 'that year of now done darkness'.

★   ★   ★

What Hopkins and Gascoyne have both finally been suggesting is that their despair may have been for a purpose. In them, God has separated the chaff from the grain, has created 'the debris of all certainties', and their returning faith may be the stronger for it.

Many thinkers have pointed to the fact that doubt is an essential part of a durable Christian faith. Not many of us will experience the agonizing despair of people like Hopkins, St Teresa or St John of the Cross. It is perhaps the sign of outstanding religious experience that such people, who reach the heights of mystical joy, should also reach the depths of doubting despair. Not everyone is vouchsafed such exceptional experiences. For most of us, the Christian life consists of a far more moderate range of feeling. But the importance of doubt, even in more humdrum existences such as ours, should never be underestimated.

The certainties which are at times uttered by some Christians can be very off-putting to those believers whose life is made up of a mixture of doubt and faith. We sometimes feel inadequate in the face of such assurance, and wonder whether there is something wrong with our own faith. Yet perhaps it could be said that a faith which has never questioned itself has never been put to the test – and that a faith that has been put to the test may be in the event much stronger, and more capable of standing up to the more harrowing experiences of life. Indeed, if it were easy to have faith, what would be the virtue in having it?

One of the poets who best expresses his own experience of the mixture of faith and doubt is R.S. Thomas.[25] Only too often, his search for God seems to lead to nothingness. There is a recurrent image, at all stages of his poetic career, of a priest praying in an empty church, unanswered. At times, however, that bleak image is lightened by the vision of the cross breaking through the silence of God, as the praying man comes to see the love of God. But, only too often, what he experiences is emptiness. The priest 'tests his faith on emptiness', nailing his questions to an 'untenanted cross' ('In Church'). The poet has almost given up the search for truth. He finds himself wishing that there were a simple 'explanation for the silence of God' ('Correspondence').

There has been a tendency among some Christian commentators to see a reassuring development in Thomas's writing, from doubt to faith, from perceived absence to perceived presence. Yet in fact, if there is a development of any kind in Thomas's verse, it is towards an even greater realization of uncertainty, a perception that there are no clear answers. When he pronounces the name of God, it is as though he is leaning over 'an immense depth', waiting 'somewhere between faith and doubt' ('Waiting') for the echoes to come back to him.

25. For a short note on R.S. Thomas, see p. 116.

The paradoxical truth is that certainty is only to be found in uncertainty, faith in doubt. In one of his parables, Jesus talked about the man who built his house upon sand, and the man who built his upon rock. When the bad weather came, the house built on sand was washed away, but the house built on rock stood firm. When we come to interpret that parable, what is sand, and what is rock? I would venture to suggest that the sand on which one house was built was the sand of false, untested certainties, which create a faith that fails at the first real test; and that the rock on which the other house was built was the rock of doubt, of uncertainty, the rock of that questioning which can create a firm, rock-like faith which can prevail against anything that may assail it.

John Habgood, in a book suitably called *Faith and Uncertainty* (1997), stresses that in order to be true to ourselves, we must accept 'the need to live and grapple with uncertainty, to find ways of being faithful without presuming to know all the answers'.[26] In an age in which most religions, including Christianity, appear to be sliding more and more in the direction of fundamentalism, this is perhaps a timely warning.

26. John Habgood, *Faith and Uncertainty* (London: Darton, Longman and Todd, 1997), p. 7.

CHAPTER EIGHT

Love

Love bade me welcome: yet my soul drew back,
  Guilty of dust and sin.
But quick-eyed Love, observing me grow slack
  From my first entrance in,
Drew nearer to me, sweetly questioning
  If I lacked anything.

A guest, I answered, worthy to be here:
  Love said, You shall be he.
I, the unkind, ungrateful? Ah my dear,
  I cannot look on thee.
Love took my hand, and smiling did reply,
  Who made the eyes but I?

Truth Lord, but I have marred them: let my shame
  Go where it doth deserve.
And know you not, says Love, who bore the blame?
  My dear, then I will serve.
You must sit down, says Love, and taste my meat:
  So I did sit and eat.

(George Herbert, 'Love')

George Herbert (1593–1633) was born of a prominent mid-Wales family. He was educated at Westminster, and Trinity College, Cambridge, where he became a Fellow. He was ordained deacon in 1626, and priest in 1630, when he was presented with the living of Bemerton in Wiltshire. He died three years later. His poetry was published posthumously through the exertions of his close friend Nicholas Ferrar of Little Gidding, under the title *The Temple*. This proved extremely popular, 13 editions coming out in the next 45 years. His contemporaries were moved by the simple piety of his poetry; later generations have, however, noted the intellectual subtlety that underlies that apparent simplicity.

This is the poem with which George Herbert rounded off the major section, 'The Church' (160 poems), of his great collection *The Temple* (1633). It is a summing-up of all that has been contained in the rest of the collection. For Herbert, God's love presents us with the meaning of all things in this life and the next. This poem places that love in the context of the reception of the human spirit at the heavenly supper at the end of time, at which the blessed will sit and eat, as described in St Luke's Gospel:

Blessed are those servants, whom the lord when he cometh shall find watching: verily I say unto you, that he shall gird himself, and make them to sit down to meat, and will come forth and serve them.

(Luke 12.37)

Another description of the same event is that, in Revelation, of the 'marriage supper of the Lamb'. At that supper, the author of Revelation is told not to prostrate himself, because, as a voice from heaven says, 'I am thy fellowservant' (Revelation 19.9–10).

Herbert's poem starts with Love welcoming the human soul, who, however, like the writer of Revelation, sees himself as unworthy, and talks of the need for a worthy guest at the feast. When Love says that he is to be that guest, he stresses once more his unworthiness, so much so that he cannot even look at Love. It is the last stanza, however, that brings out the whole meaning of the poem. Man has 'marred' the gifts he has been given by God, but Jesus Christ has 'borne the blame' on our behalf. Still convinced of his unworthiness, the poet offers to serve at table; but, in the very words from St Luke quoted above, Love tells him to 'sit down' to taste his 'meat'. We are also reminded, by the fact that it is Love that says this, of the famous passage from St John's Gospel where Jesus exhorts his disciples to love one another, and tells them that they are not his 'servants':

This is my commandment, That ye love one another, as I have loved you.
Greater love hath no man than this, that a man lay down his life for his friends.
Ye are my friends, if ye do whatsoever I command you.
Henceforth I call you not servants; for the servant knoweth not what his lord doeth: but I have called you friends; for all things that I have heard of my Father I have made known unto you.

(John 15.12–15)

There are, of course, a great many other overtones in this poem, as there are in the biblical passages on which so much of it is based. The most obvious of those overtones relates to the 'agape', or common religious meal that was in use in the early Church, which symbolized the perfect love, or 'agape', of Christians for each other.

The poem ends simply and dramatically with the phrase 'So I did sit and eat.' It is as though this has now become the most natural thing in the world, and all his doubts and uncertainties have gone.

Herbert leaves us with a heartening message. If we believe in the mission of Jesus Christ, then we are bound also to believe in the overwhelming nature of God's love for us. Love, in Herbert's poem, dismisses the poet's claim of his unworthiness by invoking Christ's sacrifice, whereby he 'bore the blame':

> For God so loved the world, that he gave his only begotten Son, that whosoever believeth in him should not perish, but have everlasting life.
> For God sent not his Son into the world to condemn the world; but that the world through him might be saved.
>
> (John 3.16–17)

This is the main theme, not just of this poem, but also of the whole final section of Herbert's collection. The four poems which precede 'Love' are concerned with the end of life, their titles being 'Death', 'Doomsday', 'Judgement' and 'Heaven'. Significantly, however, there is no mention of 'Hell'. It is as though 'Love' has taken its place. Moreover, the forbidding titles of these poems belie the nature of their content. In the poem 'Judgement', for example, Herbert talks of other people's fears at the prospect of the Almighty Judge, but tells God that, unlike them, he will not present him with pages that tell of his own merits, but will 'thrust a Testament into thy hand'. When God reads it, he will find that 'my faults are thine.' This confidence, in face of centuries of teaching by the Church about the Last Judgement and the dangers of eternal Hell, makes one wonder whether Herbert had in any way, when in Cambridge, come under the influence of those Cambridge figures who were beginning to question the doctrine of eternal torment.[27]

God's love, then, means for Herbert that we should have no fear of God's judgement. All we need to do is accept the offering that Christ has made to us.

★   ★   ★

Love is a reciprocal matter, however. In the two great Commandments, God has told us *our* duties of love: to love God himself, and to love our neighbours as ourselves. Jesus, in the passage of St John's Gospel we have seen above, exhorts his disciples to 'love one another, as I have loved you.' Human love is a reflection of divine love. As we have seen, Traherne believes human love to be the one way, in this unregenerate world, that we can create 'Heaven on Earth below'.[28]

One of the great questions, throughout the ages, has been the nature of the relationship between human and divine love. To look at this, it will be worth starting with Edmund Spenser's sonnet 'Most glorious Lord of life':

27. For information about this, see D.P. Walker, *The Decline of Hell: Seventeenth-century Discussions of Eternal Torment* (London: Routledge and Kegan Paul, 1964).
28. See p. 124.

Most glorious Lord of life, that on this day,
Didst make thy triumph over death and sin:
And having harrow'd hell, didst bring away
Captivity thence captive us to win:
  This joyous day, dear Lord, with joy begin,
And grant that we for whom thou diddest die
Being with thy dear blood clean washt from sin,
May live for ever in felicity.
  And that thy love we weighing worthily,
May likewise love thee for the same again:
And for thy sake that all like dear didst buy,
With love may one another entertain.
  So let us love, dear love, like as we ought,
Love is the lesson which the Lord us taught.

Edmund Spenser (*c.*1552–99) was born in London, and
educated at Merchant Taylors' School and Pembroke
Hall, Cambridge. While still at Cambridge, he made
translations of Petrarch and Du Bellay. His later love
poetry was in both of the main 'pure love' traditions:
the Neoplatonic tradition typified by Du Bellay's
L'Olive, and the Petrarchan tradition. His two major
works were *The Shepheardes Calender* (1579) and
The Faerie Queene (1590–96). He died in 1599, and
was buried in Westminster Abbey, his monument
describing him as 'The Prince of Poets in his Tyme'.

This glorious sonnet might seem at first sight inapplicable
to our quest, because it is essentially a secular love poem. It
appears, as Sonnet LXVIII, in the middle of Spenser's love
collection, published in 1595, entitled the *Amoretti*. Like

most Renaissance sonnet cycles of love poetry, the *Amoretti* uses a whole variety of sources to illustrate the poet's love, which is depicted as a pure love in the Neoplatonic tradition (that love of a perfect object can bring back to us a memory of the 'forms' or 'Idea' of perfection that existed in the perfect world from which we have fallen into the material world around us). Amid the many other sonnets in the collection, this one alone uses Christian imagery, which may seem out of place to us, but was not so to the Renaissance mind. Love poets in this period, particularly in Italy and France, made extensive use of Christian imagery in order to promote their love. Christian imagery in fact fits in well with the 'pure love' traditions (the Platonic idea, for example, of an ideal world which is merely reflected in our material world, being very much in harmony with Christian beliefs). Often, references to the great Christian festivals led into celebration of 'perfect' human love. This is what Spenser is doing in this poem, with the theme of Easter Day. He ends by persuading his beloved, 'dear love', that she should love him. Just as, in erotic poetry, the poet persuades his mistress to give in to him by drawing attention to the passing of time and the fading of beauty, in order to say 'Let us then love each other', so here Spenser persuades his beloved ('dear love') to share his 'pure love', by arguing from the teachings of Christ:

So let us love, dear love, like as we ought,
Love is the lesson which the Lord us taught.

Despite its secular nature, this poem does however tell us important things about the relationship between human and divine love. The words can, in that sense, transcend the context. And, as so many modern critics tell us, the text is

151

what matters (taking on a life of its own), not the intention of the writer.

If we ignore the references to the poet's beloved, this poem in fact contains a clear exposition of the idea of agape, that love of Christians for one another which mirrors the love of God. This is the 'charity' to which St Paul refers in his chapter on 'faith, hope and charity' in Chapter 13 of his First Epistle to the Corinthians. The early Christians used these two words, the Greek *agape* and the Latin *caritas*, in order to distinguish this divine form of love from other forms, such as *eros* or sensual love. It is 'agape' of which the two Great Commandments speak, when we are told to love God, and to love our neighbour.

Yet we can surely go beyond this. Spenser's use of the concept of agape in order to further his love for one individual woman is not entirely out of place. In one interpretation, all forms of human love can be seen as reflections of divine love. Henri Lacordaire (1802–61), the famous nineteenth-century French Dominican preacher, once said: 'There are not two kinds of love.' What he meant is that human love and divine love are of the same essence, and that we create, by our actions on earth, a kind of incomplete reflection of God's divine and perfect love for us. So our human kind of love for another human being teaches us something important about the love of God for us, and the love we should give to God.

★   ★   ★

So let us return to that question of God's love for us. We have seen George Herbert's trust that, when we are judged at the end of time, God's love will sustain us. This is echoed in one of Emily Dickinson's most evocative poems:

'Unto Me?' I do not know you –
Where may be your House?

'I am Jesus – Late of Judaea –
Now – of Paradise' –

Wagons – have you – to convey me?
This is far from Thence –

'Arms of Mine – sufficient Phaeton –
Trust Omnipotence' –

I am spotted – 'I am Pardon' –
I am small – 'The Least
Is esteemed in Heaven the Chiefest –
Occupy my House' –

The first line of this poem echoes the passage from St
Matthew's Gospel which became the first of the 'Comfortable
Words' in the 1662 prayer book: 'Come unto me all that
travail and are heavy laden, and I will refresh you' (Matthew
11.28). Given what we have seen of Dickinson's emotional
condition,[29] those comforting words, in which Christ is
calling out to all those suffering from grief and depression,
must have meant much to her. Yet her first words claim that
they cannot refer to her: 'Unto me? I do not know you.'
Jesus replies to her, in prosaic terms; he is 'late of Judaea',
but now 'of Paradise'. Again, the words provide us with an
allusion to other words of Christ's – the 'today shalt thou be
with me in Paradise' said to the thief dying alongside him
on the Cross. Already the main theme of the poem, Christ's
forgiveness of sinners, is foreshadowed.

29. See pp. 128–32.

To all Dickinson's objections, Jesus answers with reassuring words, which remind us of other biblical statements. To the question of how she is to be conveyed to his 'House' in Paradise, which is so far off (though the image is physical, the implication is that it is far off not physically, but through her unworthiness), Jesus echoes the reassuring words from Deuteronomy, 'The eternal God is thy refuge, and underneath are the everlasting arms' (Deuteronomy 33.27) – which are particularly well known because they form one of the 'sentences' pronounced by a priest as he precedes the coffin into the church for a funeral service. Jesus's 'arms' are a 'sufficient Phaeton' (a 'phaeton' being a four-wheeled carriage – note again how the spiritual message is being conveyed through banal material imagery). He must be trusted, in his omnipotence.

Now we come to the true reason for her reluctance to believe that she will be accepted: 'I am spotted', in other words I am full of sin. This echoes the biblical word for sin in the Authorized Version (e.g., 'the garment spotted by the flesh', Jude 23, or 'Be diligent that ye may be found of him in peace, without spot, and blameless', 2 Peter 3.14). The word 'spotted' plays much the same role here as the word 'marred' in Herbert's poem. Christ's response is immediate and direct: 'I am Pardon.' Next, she claims her insignificance: 'I am small.' Again, the response is direct and immediate. Echoing the Beatitudes, 'Blest are the poor in spirit: for theirs is the kingdom of heaven' (Matthew 5.3), he assures her that in heaven the least become the greatest. He then tells her to 'occupy my House.' The use of the word 'House' at the beginning and end of the poem reminds us of the image used by Christ to describe the eternal life of the just: 'In my Father's house are many mansions' (John 14.2).

In its simple depiction of a dialogue with Christ, this

154

poem assures us of God's love for us all. His 'everlasting arms' are always there to lift us up, and he is our refuge. Our sins have been redeemed by his loving sacrifice, and, like the thief on the cross, we will be accepted into Paradise, where the first shall be last and the last shall be first.

★   ★   ★

Love is a good note on which to end this book, in which we have meditated on a number of the mysteries of God's relationship with humankind. If we look back on the journey we have taken, we will find that running through everything, through trials and tribulations as well as joys, there is the constant presence of God's love for us. If we reciprocate that love, 'so amazing, so divine' that it 'demands my soul, my life, my all', we will learn to deal with all that the world can throw at us. We will also, by reflecting that love of God in our love for our neighbours, help, in Traherne's words, to create 'Heaven on Earth below'.

Further Reading

Individual poets

(This selection is not restricted to the poets used in this volume. In each case the edition I have found it easiest to find has been listed.)

Blake, William, *The Lyrical Poems* (ed. Walter Raleigh; Oxford: The Clarendon Press, 1905).

Chesterton, G.K., *Stories, Essays and Poems* (London: J.M. Dent, 1935).

Clare, John, *Selected Poems* (London; Penguin Books, 1990).

Dickinson, Emily, *The Collected Poems* (ed. Thomas H. Johnson; London: Faber and Faber, 1975).

Donne, John, *Complete English Poems* (ed. C.A. Patrides and Robin Hamilton; London: Dent/Everyman, 1994).

Eliot, T.S., *Collected Poems, 1909–1962* (London: Faber and Faber, 1974).

Fletcher, Giles, *The Complete Poems* (ed. the Revd Alexander B. Grosart; London: Chatto and Windus, 1876).

Gascoyne, David, *Collected Poems 1988* (Oxford and New York: Oxford University Press, 1988).

Herbert, George, *The English Poems* (ed. C.A. Patrides; London: Dent/Everyman, 1974).

Hill, Geoffrey, *Collected Poems* (London: Penguin Books, 1985).

Hopkins, Gerard Manley, *Poetry and Prose* (ed. Walford Davies; London: Dent/Everyman, 1998).

Humphreys, Emyr, *Collected Poems* (Cardiff: University of Wales Press, 1999).

Johnson, Lionel, *The Complete Poems* (ed. Iain Fletcher; London: The Unicorn Press, 1953).

Lewis, Saunders, 'Selected Poems (Translated by Gwyn Thomas)', in Alun R. Jones and Gwyn Thomas (eds), *Presenting Saunders Lewis* (Cardiff: University of Wales Press, 1973).

Meynell, Alice, *Collected Poems* (London: Burns, Oates and Washbourne, 1923).

Muir, Edwin, *The Complete Poems* (ed. Peter Butler; Aberdeen: Association for Scottish Literary Studies, 1991).

Patmore, Coventry, *Poems* (ed. F. Page; London: Oxford University Press, 1949).

Péguy, Charles, *Oeuvres poétiques complètes* (Paris: Gallimard NRF (Pléiade), 1960).

Raine, Kathleen, *The Collected Poems* (Ipswich: Golgonooza Press, 2000).

Southwell, Robert, *Poems* (ed. J.H. McDonald and Nancy P. Brown; Oxford: Clarendon Press, 1967).

Spenser, Edmund, *The Poetical Works* (ed. J.C. Smith and E. de Selincourt; London, New York and Toronto: Oxford University Press, 1912).

Thomas, R.S., *Collected Poems 1945–1990* (London: Phoenix Giant, 1995).

Thomas, R.S., *Collected Later Poems 1988–2000* (Tarset: Bloodaxe Books, 2004).

Thompson, Francis, *Collected Poems* (ed. Brigid Boardman; London and New York: Continuum (in association with Boston College), 2001).

Traherne, Thomas, *Centuries, Poems and Thanksgivings* (ed. H.M. Margoliouth; London: Oxford University Press, 1958).

Vaughan, Henry. *The Complete Poems* (ed. Alan Rudrum; London: Penguin Books, 1983).

Watts, Isaac, *Works*. (2 vols, ed. G. Burder; London: John Barfield, 1811).

Anthologies, etc.

Gardner, Helen (ed.), *The Faber Book of Religious Verse* (London: Faber Paperbacks, 1979).

Nicholson, Norman (ed.), *An Anthology of Religious Verse, Designed for the times* (London: Pelican Books, 1942).

Pryce, Mark (ed.) *Literary Companion to the Lectionary* (London: SPCK, 2001).

Pryce, Mark (ed.), *Literary Companion for Festivals* (London: SPCK, 2003).

Quinn, Michael, *Covenant with Silence* (n.d. [2005]).

Thomas, R.S. (ed.), *The Penguin Book of Religious Verse* (London: Penguin Books, 1963).

Other Sources

Andrewes, Lancelot, 'A Cold Coming', in John Chandos (ed.), *In God's Name: Examples of Preaching in England from the Act of Supremacy to the Act of Uniformity, 1534–1662* (Indianapolis: Bobbs-Merrill, 1971).

Barnes, Julian, *A History of the World in 10^1/$_2$ Chapters* (London: Jonathan Cape, 1989).

Cingria, Alexandre, *La Décadence de l'art sacré* (Paris: Bibliothèque de l'Art Catholique, 1999).

Duployé, Pie, OP, *La Littérature dans le Royaume de Dieu* (Paris: Bibliothèque de l'Homme d'Action, 1961).

Farrer, Austin, *Love Almighty and Ills Unlimited: An Essay on Providence and Evil* (New York: Doubleday, 1961).

Fenton, John, *St Matthew (The Penguin New Testament Commentaries)* (London: Penguin Books, 1963).

Habgood, John, *Faith and Uncertainty* (London: Darton Longman and Todd, 1997).

Harries, Richard, *God outside the Box: Why Spiritual People Object to Christianity* (London: SPCK, 2002).

Huxley, Aldous, *Brave New World* (London: Chatto and Windus, 1932).

Proust, Marcel, *A la recherche du temps perdu* (trans. Moncrieff and Kilmartin; London: Folio Society, 1982).

Runcie, Robert, 'Zeebrugge Ferry Disaster', in John F. Thornton and Katharine Washburn (eds), *The Times Greatest Sermons of the Last 2000 Years* (London: HarperCollins, 1999).

Sacks, Rabbi Jonathan, Article in *The Times*, 8 January 2005.

Thomas, R.S., *Selected Prose* (ed. Sandra Anstey; Bridgend: Poetry Wales Press, 1983).

Walker, D.P., *The Decline of Hell: Seventeenth-century Discussions of Eternal Torment* (London: Routledge and Kegan Paul, 1964).

Ward, Keith, *God, Faith and the New Millennium: Christian Belief in an Age of Science* (New York: Oneworld Publications, 1998).